Town Walks

in

Devon

Simone Stanbrook–Byrne

and

James Clancy

CULM VALLEY PUBLISHING

Published by

Culm Valley Publishing Ltd
Culmcott House
Mill Street, Uffculme
Cullompton, Devon
EX15 3AT, UK
Tel: +44(0)1884 849085
Fax: +44(0)1884 840251
E-mail: info@culmvalleypublishing.co.uk
Website: www.culmvalleypublishing.co.uk

First published 2012

ISBN 978-1-907942-05-1 paperback

British Library Cataloguing-in-Publication Data
A catalogue record for this book is available from the British Library

Typeset by Culm Valley Publishing Ltd
Printed and bound by T.J. International Ltd, Padstow, Cornwall

Front cover image: The Great House and Slee's Almshouses, Tiverton
Back cover image: The Duke of Bedford's statue, Tavistock
All images used in this book are available as cards and prints from Culm Valley Publishing

Contents

Introduction

Throughout this book the directions for the walks are in black type enabling them to be picked out easily.

The history notes are in green italics. Of necessity, the history snippets are brief, designed to whet the appetite and encourage more research if you so desire.

Although we often start the walks from car parks, public transport access is given for each route.

Our sketch maps are not to scale. Used in conjunction with the text you should end up back where you started.

On any walk in town or country common sense must prevail: be properly shod, take care where you put your feet and be prepared for the weather. Although these walks are in towns and therefore close to amenities, it may be an idea to take food and first aid supplies plus a mobile phone.

We have thoroughly enjoyed preparing these routes of exploration – we hope you enjoy following them.

People's Park, Tiverton

Disclaimer

Points that should be borne in mind:

Landmarks and buildings can change: buildings are demolished, new ones appear, road junctions change etc. In such cases a modicum of common sense must be exercised to keep yourself on the route, but we are always pleased to be advised of such changes.

Pavements and roads are usually well-maintained but please watch your step, accidents happen easily.

Watch out for traffic — please don't get mown down whilst stepping back to admire a building.

We hope that you enjoy these walks without mishap, but urge you to exercise caution at all times. Neither the authors nor Culm Valley Publishing Ltd. accept responsibility for any misadventure which may occur during or arise from these walks and suggested routes.

Acknowledgements
Our grateful thanks to:

Tony Byrne
Nic, Ella and William Clancy
John Cochrane, Colyton Parish History Society
Andora Glanville, for Dartmouth information
Catherine Hart, Churchwarden, Barnstaple Parish Church
Denise Holton, Barnstaple Heritage Centre
Karen Newman, Barnstaple Antique and Collectors' Centre
Philip Roe, for Dartmouth information
Tavistock TIC

Exploring the catacombs, Exeter

The Esplanade, Sidmouth

Walk Locations

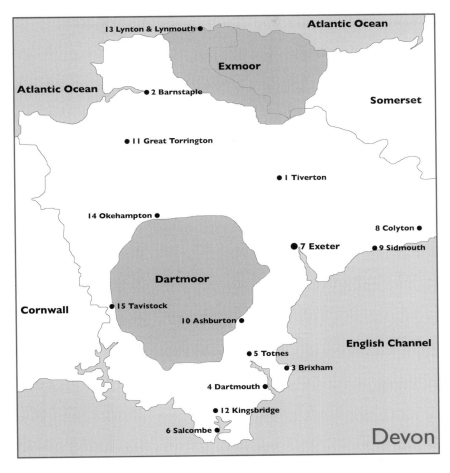

Tiverton
Distance: 2½ miles / 4km

Tiverton is an historic market town nestling amongst hills in the Exe Valley. Its name derives from 'Twy-ford-ton' meaning the town on two fords, as the rivers Exe and Lowman meet here. Tiverton has endured many major fires down the centuries but despite this much history remains. During the course of this mostly level walk, particularly during the latter part, you will see plaques, placed by the Civic Society. Look out for these as they give excellent history snippets about the buildings you are passing. A very short stretch of Martins Lane is unsurfaced.

Start point: Multi-storey car park on Phoenix Lane, EX16 6PP

Directions to start: Tiverton is situated in Mid Devon on the A396, 15 miles north of Exeter

Parking: Long-stay, multi-storey car park at the bottom of Phoenix Lane (pay & display)

Public transport: Tiverton is well-served by buses from Exeter (Stagecoach Devon) and Taunton (First). Timetables available online at www.travelinesw.com. The nearest railway station is Tiverton Parkway (5 miles)

Refreshments: The Flying Pickle, 40 Gold Street, 01884 242661; Four & Twenty Blackbirds, 43 Gold Street, 01884 257055; Mallards, 3 Lowman Green, 01884 252258; White Ball Inn, 8 Bridge Street, 01884 251525

Toilets: Lowman Green, Market Square, People's Park and Phoenix Lane

Nearby places to stay: Angel Guest House, 01884 253392; Howden House B&B, 01884 253132

Places of interest: Tiverton Canal Company (horse-drawn barge trips), Canal Hill, 01884 253345; Tiverton Castle, Park Hill, 01884 253200 / 255200; Tiverton Museum, Beck's Square, 01884 256295

Market days: Tuesday (main) / Friday / Saturday

Authors' tip: If time allows we recommend a trip to the National Trust property of Knightshayes Court, 2 miles north of Tiverton at Bolham

Leave the car park by the main pedestrian exit on the north side. Cross the road, passing the roundabout on your left and walk up Phoenix Lane. A well-stocked TIC is on your left and soon you reach the Burma Star Association Memorial Garden on the right and the Rotary Club Wishing Well on the left.

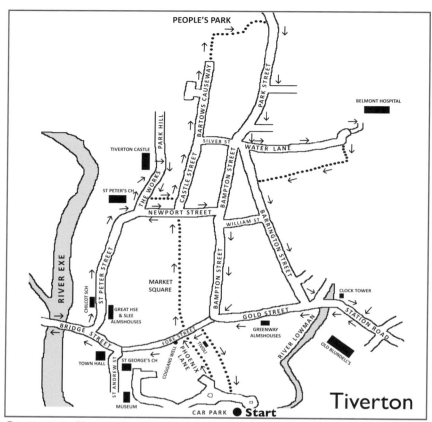

Tiverton

Continue up Phoenix Lane until it meets Fore Street at a T-junction. Here bear very slightly left to see the bubbling-up Coggan's Well at the edge of the pavement. This marks the termination of the Town Leat.

The Town Leat: *During the 13thC the townspeople of Tiverton were given a water supply known as the Town Leat. Every seven years a ceremonial 'Perambulation of the Leat' occurs, during which hundreds of people follow the Leat from Coggan's Well to its source north of Tiverton at Norwood Common, about 6 miles away*

Cross over Fore Street and bear right to enter the passageway into Tiverton Pannier Market. Emerge into the market square and walk straight ahead through the market buildings. Beyond the buildings pass Market Walk on your right and continue ahead through the car park to leave the market square beside Clare House Surgery.

Market Square: *Evidence of human occupation of this area dates back to the Stone Age. As the town developed over the centuries so the market grew up and flourished. By 1200 Tiverton had a regular market and several annual fairs. Reputedly the site of a former Roman camp, the Grade II listed building you see now was built in 1830. It was restored and re-opened in 2006*

Turn left along Newport Street. The Baptist Church is on the right and ahead you will see the magnificent St. Peter's Church. Go through its lychgate and explore the churchyard and the building itself – it's well worth allowing time to do this.

St. Peter's Church: *Consecrated in 1073, this church is a tapestry of history and architecture. The Norman doorway on the north side is the oldest part while the lovely, light Greenway Chapel was funded by John Greenway, a wool merchant, in the early 16thC. The lion and unicorn on the Mayor's Pew date from 1615. Notice the intricate chandelier, which cost £67 in 1707. The colourful array of kneelers are a cheerful, modern addition*

Leave the church porch and bear left part-way round the building to the corner of the churchyard by the road and Tiverton Castle, where you find an exit gate. Beyond here you will notice a rather substantial wooden bus shelter, erected by the Heathcoat Trust in 1958. You will also see the buildings of Tiverton Castle, a private home but open to the public at certain times. Walk along the road a little way to admire its façade.

Tiverton Castle *was originally a 'motte and bailey' construction dating from the 12thC. It was rebuilt and enlarged during the Middle Ages when still under the ownership of the Earls of Devon. Since the 16thC it has had a succession of owners. Its eventful involvement in the English Civil War during the 17thC eventually gave way to more peaceful times. The castle is still in private ownership and makes for a fascinating visit*

Return to the bus shelter and cross the road (carefully) towards Castle View Dental Practice. Pass round the right hand end of this building and bear immediately left to find a tiny, narrow footpath between the dental practice and the beer garden of The Queen's Head. This is Hit or Miss Alley and takes you through to Castle Street.

Hit or Miss Alley *is the site of the old tilt yard where the castle garrison once practised jousting. The name was later corrupted to 'Hippopotamus'*

Turn left along Castle Street following the direction of the Leat which flows along the middle of the road. At the end of Castle Street keep straight ahead along Bartows Causeway.

At the end of Bartows Causeway pass through the gates and enter People's Park. A short path of 50m or so leads to a T-junction. The park is a lovely place for a stroll and a picnic and boasts a very tempting playground, which we found difficult to resist! The walk turns right at the T-junction along the edge of the park to leave by some rather splendid wrought iron gates adjacent to the old park keeper's house. Notice the inscription on the outside of the gateposts.

> **People's Park** *was formed in 1887 to celebrate Queen Victoria's golden jubilee. It was opened to the public in July 1888. An American War Memorial has recently been installed near the north end of the park*

Emerge from the park and turn right along Park Road passing Belmont Road on your left. The road becomes Park Street and soon you meet a junction with Silver Street to the right and Bampton Street ahead. Turn left here, away from Silver Street, and follow the narrow Water Lane, ignoring Barrington Street to the right. We are now exploring some of the narrow backwaters of Tiverton. Water Lane leads to a T-Junction of paths. Go left, then follow the path as it bends right and passes through a stone gateway, to get a glimpse of the now derelict Belmont Hospital. At the time of writing the eeriness of the scene was more reminiscent of a POW camp than a hospital.

> **Belmont Hospital** *was originally a Victorian Workhouse. The present Grade II listed building dates from 1837 and is on the site of an earlier workhouse. It was built to accommodate 300 people and cost in the region of £6,000. After WWII it became a geriatric hospital. Various plans have been suggested to redevelop the area for residential use*

Retrace through the stone gate this time bearing left with the lane. Pass the entrance to Water Lane and now keep ahead on the trodden earth path with houses on the right. After 35m the path curves round to the right, continue along it for a further 170m to emerge on Barrington Street where a sign shows that the final stretch of path you've just followed was Martins Lane.

Turn left along Barrington Street and keep ahead for 280m, passing Castle Primary School on your left and William Street on your right, until you reach the T-junction with Gold Street.

St. Peter's Church

Town Hall

Old Blundell's

Castle Street

Once on Gold Street turn left towards the clock tower and cross the road with care to the statue of Edward the Peacemaker on the bridge. This area of town is Lowman Green and the body of water here is the River Lowman, one of the two rivers whose fords gave Tiverton its name. If you wish you can wander down to the river where hungry ducks usually await.

The Clock Tower: *Another Grade II listed building dating from 1907/8. It was donated to the town by Mr. T Ford, a former mayor and magistrate, who bought the site for £50. Some years ago the people of Tiverton awoke one April 1st to find a sign high up on the tower: "Sold for export to the USA". The local estate agents are not averse to the odd practical joke – always reassuring!*

Continue along the road as it bends right by the clock tower. Follow the stone wall until you reach an arched stone gateway. Through this can be found the impressive building of the original Blundell's School.

Old Blundell's School *was founded in 1604 with money and land left by Peter Blundell, who died in 1601. His initials can be seen today on the weather vane mounting the clock tower. During his lifetime he become a wealthy merchant amassing his fortune principally in the cloth industry. One famous ex-Blundellian was the author R. D. Blackmore. In the first chapter of 'Lorna Doone' he used the triangular lawn here as the stage for a fight between John Ridd and Robin Snell. In May 1882 the whole school relocated to a new site at Horsdon, a mile outside the town. The school has always been highly regarded and remains so today*

Turn away from the gate and head back into town to re-cross the Lowman. From here continue along Gold Street where, in approx 100m, you'll see the fabulous old building of Greenway Almshouses on your left.

Almshouses *in Tiverton have a long history. They were built by wealthy benefactors to house the poor. The Greenway Almshouses and Chapel were the first in the town, built by John Greenway and dating back to the 1520s when they housed 5 poor men. The chapel survived the fire of 1731. The Slee's Almshouses on St. Peter Street were built in memory of George Slee's daughter, Eleanor, who died in the fire of 1598*

Continue past Banbury's department store on your left. Keep ahead here into the pedestrianised Fore Street, ignoring Bampton Street to the right. In 200m you reach the quite magnificent building of the Town Hall. Just before it you will find St. George's Church on your left which is Grade I Listed and one of the best Georgian churches in the county.

The road to the left between St. George's and the Town Hall is St. Andrew's Street. This leads to access to the Tiverton Museum of Mid Devon Life which is well worth visiting, but the walk continues ahead, past the Town Hall and Memorial Hall to descend to the River Exe. Pause awhile on the bridge: the view north upriver, graced by swans, the tower of St. Peter's Church above the trees and the fields beyond Tiverton, is worth admiring.

Turn away from the river and retrace your steps back uphill, this time bearing left up Angel Hill away from the Town Hall to enter St. Peter Street. Look up to your right to see the lovely old Slee's Almshouses and The Great House (see cover pic). On your left is the edifice of the United Reformed Church followed by the old Chilcott School, now an auction house.

The Great House of St. George: *This imposing, Grade II* listed building was built for George Slee, a wealthy wool merchant, at the start of the 17thC. It was built to replace his previous home, destroyed in 1598 by one of Tiverton's many great fires. It was damaged by fire in 1731 and restored. It has also served as a doctor's surgery and later as offices for Mid Devon District Council who undertook more restoration during the late 1990s. It has been owned by a private company since 2004*

Chilcot School *was founded by Robert Chilcot, nephew of Peter Blundell, principally for the teaching of reading and writing. The current building was constructed in 1611. It survived the fire of 1612 and remained operational as a school until 1906. It now houses Chilcotts the Auctioneers, though the name here reflects the current owners of the business, who bear no relation to Robert Chilcot*

Walk up St. Peter Street passing the Methodist Church on the right and admiring the many beautiful buildings. As the road bends you'll once again see St. Peter's Church ahead of you.

At the end of St. Peter Street turn right into Newport Street and retrace your steps a short distance, passing the entrance to the market on your right. At the traffic lights turn right into Bampton Street towards the end of which you'll pass the attractive pillared shop fronts of the old Market House on your right.

The Market House *was built in 1732 and opened on market days for the sale of corn. John Wesley, largely credited for forming the Methodist movement and known for his open-air preaching, gave sermons here on eight occasions between 1750 and 1765. It was converted to the style you see today in 1971*

When you reach Gold Street, with Banbury's ahead, turn right for a short distance looking out for the second passageway on the left. This is almost opposite the entrance to the pannier market which you went through earlier. Turn left through this passageway glimpsing the facia of the Tivoli cinema over the wall on your right. At the end of this path you emerge opposite a car park. Turn right to return to the roundabout by the multi-storey from whence you started.

Tivoli Cinema: *The Art Deco style Tivoli held the distinction of being the oldest independent cinema in the country when it closed its doors in 2007. It was, thankfully, saved as a cinema when new owners, Merlin Cinemas, reopened it in June 2008*

Looking north along the River Exe towards St. Peter's

Barnstaple
Distance: 2 miles / 3.2km

Barnstaple has some beautiful buildings and a wealth of history. During the 11thC it had its own mint and during the Middle Ages it was a staple port for the export of wool, a trade which brought great wealth to the town. Many of the buildings you see today, including the market, the clock tower and Bridge Chambers, were designed by Richard Gould. This is an easy, level route, the only hill being encountered if you decide on the brief excursion to the top of the castle mound at the end of the walk.

Start point: Cattle Market Car Park, Holland Street, EX31 1DP

Directions to start: Barnstaple is situated in North Devon, 34 miles north west of Exeter. Major roads that converge on the town are the A39, A361 and A377

Parking: Cattle Market Car Park, Holland Street

Public transport: There are numerous bus connections to and from Barnstaple with services run by FirstGroup and Stagecoach Devon amongst others. Timetables available online at www.travelinesw.com. Barnstaple railway station is located at Station Road

Refreshments: The Cream Tea Café, Church Lane, 01271 325727; Driftwood Café, Gammon Walk, 01271 329488

Toilets: Cattle Market Car Park and pannier market

Nearby places to stay: The Imperial Hotel, Taw Vale Parade, 01271 345861; The Old Post Office, 22 Pilton Street, 01271 859439; Sunnymead B&B, 2 Sunnymead, 01271 325254

Places of interest: Arlington Court (NT) and the National Trust Carriage Museum, Arlington, 01271 850296; Broomhill Sculpture Gardens, Muddiford, 01271 850262; Museum of Barnstaple and North Devon, The Square, 01271 346747

Market days: General market: Tuesday, Friday and Saturday. Craft and General Market: Monday (April to Christmas) and Thursday; Antiques & Collectables: Wednesday

Authors' tip: Consider a 3-mile excursion to visit Broomhill Sculpture Gardens with its 300+ sculptures in 10 acres of gardens. It also has a fabulous restaurant plus accommodation (see 'places of interest' above)

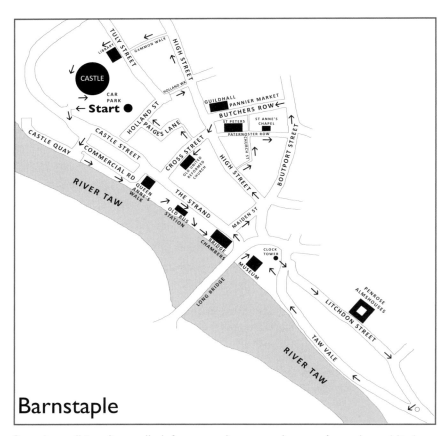

Barnstaple

Start by walking diagonally left across the car park, away from the public loos and towards a red brick building with rounded walls. When you reach the road by this building cross over and turn left – you will see a pub called Monkey Island on your left. Pass the old station building on the right and go right beyond it towards the River Taw. Lean on the railings and look right towards the clean lines of the modern bridge, then turn left and walk along the path towards the lovely old bridge which dates back to the 15thC. Keep the river to your right.

> **Bridge:** *The old bridge, also known as 'Long Bridge' is first mentioned in records dating back to around the 13thC. It has been modified and widened over the centuries*

A little way along you will find the colonnaded building of Queen Anne's Walk (the colonnades are on the side away from you as you approach). Turn left here to walk past its front, then go right along the road (Castle Street) as far as The Old Bus Station, once a railway station, on the right. Admire its façade then turn right to re-join the riverside path, continuing with the river on your right and passing behind the grand buildings of the Bridge Chambers on your left. Walk under the old bridge, then go left up some steps immediately after it. These lead to the Museum of Barnstaple and North Devon, which also houses an information centre. At the end of the building turn right towards the clock tower which was built as a memorial to Prince Albert in 1862 and was restored in 2009.

Queen Anne's Walk *was once a merchant's 'exchange' adjacent to the quay. Dating back to the early 18thC, it is Grade I listed and is on the site of an earlier exchange. The building behind the colonnades was built in 1850 and has had a variety of uses including that of bath house and Masonic lodge*

Brannam's Pottery (top left); Long Bridge (top right); Queen Anne's Walk (above)

Clock Tower   St. Peter's Church

Great Quay *was built in 1550 and was situated in front of Queen Anne's Walk. In the 16th–17thC Barnstaple was a great centre of commerce, importing wine, tobacco and spices as well as boodle from privateering! The main export products were wool and pottery. Great Quay was one of the facilities built to accommodate the ships which plied their trade and from here, in 1588, five ships sailed to fight the Spanish Armada. By 1850 the river was so silted up that the quay was no longer in use and so was filled in. A railway station was constructed on the site*

Continue in the same direction beyond the clock tower, crossing the road and walking ahead down Litchdon Street, the Imperial Hotel is on your right. A short way down you will find the beautiful buildings where Brannam's pottery had its being until 1990. It now houses a hairdresser's. Look up to admire the stained glass on the first floor.

Just beyond here you will find the venerable Penrose Almshouses, notice their little bell tower at the far end. Continue to the end of Litchdon Street, ignoring a road coming in from the left, and you will reach a junction with New Road and Taw Vale. Turn sharp right here and cross over towards the pinnacle which marks the end of Rock Park – one William Frederick Rock presented the park to the people in 1879. Walk away from the pinnacle, back along the river, which is to your left – you are now approaching the old bridge from its other side.

Penrose Almshouses *were founded in the 17thC by John Penrose, a successful merchant and sometime mayor who bequeathed money for their construction. The eagle-eyed might spot bullet holes dating back to the Civil War. They are Grade I listed*

There are some lovely, balconied houses to your right as you progress along here, culminating in the front façade of the Imperial Hotel. Return to the clock tower and from it walk ahead, passing the museum and information centre on your left. Cross the road and continue along the front of the Bridge Chambers. This is now The Strand. Opposite the Bridge Chambers' entrance turn right off The Strand along Maiden Street. At the end of Maiden Street glance across to The Bank restaurant, once a 17thC merchant's house. It has a fabulous ceiling if you peek inside. From Maiden Street turn left and left again up High Street and within 100m turn right along the very narrow Church Lane.

As this lane bends left notice the old school on the right followed by the Horwood Almshouses and the Paige Almshouses. Beyond here you meet a crossing of paths. Go left, this is Paternoster Row, and visit the Grade II* listed

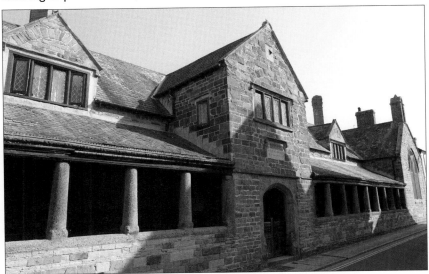

Penrose Almshouses

Church Lane

parish church of St. Peter, with its golden weather vane and twisted spire, caused by the lead warping in the heat of the sun.

Come out of the church and turn left back along Paternoster Row, walking past Church Lane and continuing ahead on the path between two ancient buildings: St. Anne's Chapel on the left and the younger Parish Hall on the right.

__Church Lane and Paternoster Row__ are teeming with history. The old Horwood School was founded in 1659 by Alice Horwood for "20 poor maids". The girls were taught to sew and read but not to write. Priorities were very different then. It functioned as a school until 1814 and the building was restored in 1917. Beyond this are the Horwood Almshouses, founded by the wealthy merchant Thomas Horwood, also in the mid 17thC, and completed by his wife. These were to house 16 people whereas the Paige's Almshouses next door, founded by Elizabeth Paige in 1656, were for just 8 residents. These were built on the site of even older almshouses. All these buildings are Grade II* listed. Beyond the almshouses the paths are surrounded by raised ground. This is due to the area having been a burial site for many centuries, with surplus soil being scattered over the ground after burials, gradually raising the level. There has been a church on the site of St. Peter's in Paternoster Row since Saxon times, the original building would have been wooden. The present church dates back to the 14thC with many successive alterations over the centuries. The Grade I *listed St.Anne's Chapel is thought to have originated in the 14thC although the crypt is much older and may once have functioned as a charnel house. The chapel building also served as a grammar school from the mid 16thC to the early 20thC. John Gay, composer of The Beggar's Opera, was educated here. The building on the opposite side of Paternoster Row from St.Anne's is now a very active Parish Hall*

At the end of the path turn left along Boutport Street, one of the main shopping areas, and within 100m go left along the quaint Butcher's Row with its Mecca of tiny, independent shops on the left hand side and the bustling pannier market on the right. Both are good for browsing. At the end of Butcher's Row notice the 1827 Guildhall on the right hand corner then turn left along High Street followed by the next right down Cross Street.

Butchers' Row *is a series of small, delightful shops built in 1855 of Bath stone. Few of them remain as butchers and nowadays they are a good source of artisan foods. Previously the butchers' market was held where The Guildhall and part of the pannier market now stand*

Pannier Market: *A market place has existed in this town since Saxon times. The pannier market building was constructed in 1855 to replace the previous outdoor market which was held along the High Street and fell short of hygiene requirements even for those days. Originally it was primarily for the sale of vegetables. The name derives from the panniers or baskets in which goods were once brought to market, long before a building such as this existed*

A short way down Cross Street you will find the Grade II listed building of the old United Reformed Church on the left. This ceased to be a church over 20 years ago and now houses an antiques centre. Their antiques are worth browsing, as is the interior of this delightful building. Leave the building, turning right to retrace your steps along Cross Street for about 30m, crossing the road and taking the first left along a narrow way until it emerges near the car park. This is Paiges Lane.

Turn right at the car park, this is Holland Street, and keep ahead as it enters the narrow Holland Walk. At the end turn left along High Street, passing the modern Green Lanes Shopping Centre on the right. Soon you reach the pedestrianised Gammon Walk on the left. Take this, first noticing the ornate façade of the shop on the corner. At the end of Gammon Walk turn right and walk past the library and record office, then turn left around the end of the building to approach the open space of Barnstaple's old motte and bailey castle. Explore the surroundings here as several information boards give interesting details about the history of the area.

A clear path winds up to the top of the castle which we recommend you ascend. You're standing on centuries of history up here although a blind eye has to be turned to any 21stC litter. Descend by the same path to walk anticlockwise around the mound and back to the car park.

__Barnstaple Castle__ was a 'motte and bailey' design, which comprised a wooden keep on a mound or 'motte' surrounded by an enclosure or 'bailey'. The first wooden castle here was 11thC with a stone building the following century, but by the 14thC the building was falling into ruin with the 'motte' being the most visible remnant today. Much of the stone was removed for building purposes elsewhere in the area. Prior to the Norman Conquest the area was an Anglo Saxon burial site

Site of the old motte and bailey castle

Brixham
Distance: 2 miles / 3.2km

This lovely seaside town is built into the hills surrounding the bay, the attractive, colourful buildings encompassing the harbour below. Brixham has developed from a medieval fishing village into a bustling, contemporary fishing port. Despite that it doesn't feel at all industrial and its history is very evident. The paths and pavements are good and most of the ascents and descents are on flights of steps which make the going up and down less strenuous. There are many viewpoints at which to pause and admire plus a huge number of places to stop for refreshment and browsing.

Start point: Breakwater Car Park, Berry Head Road TQ5 9AF

Directions to start: Brixham is on the South Devon coast, accessed off the A385 from Totnes

Parking: Breakwater Car Park, Berry Head Road (pay & display)

Public transport: Brixham is well-served by buses from nearby towns, operated by Stagecoach and various other companies. Timetables available online at www.travelinesw.com. There is no train service to Brixham, the nearest station being Paignton (3½ miles)

Refreshments: Breakwater Bistro, Berry Head Road, 01803 856738; Brixham Deli, Fore Street, 01803 859585

Toilets: Breakwater Car Park and also near the harbour

Nearby places to stay: Fair Winds Guest House, New Street, 01803 857537; Sampford Guest House, King Street, 01803 857761

Places of interest: Brixham Heritage Museum, New Road, 01803 856267; Coleton Fishacre Gardens (NT), near Kingswear, 01803 752466; The Golden Hind, The Quay, 01803 856223

Market days: Monday, Tuesday, Wednesday

Authors' tip: Allow time at the end of the walk to perambulate the breakwater to the lighthouse. This is a lovely walk out 'into the sea' and is just under half a mile in each direction

This car park is a scenic place to start the walk. Scan across the harbour and up the hillside, the tiers of multi-coloured houses are delightful and high up across the town you can see the church keeping an eye on what's going on.

On the west side of the car park (bearing in mind that the breakwater is to the north!) take the broad walkway through another area of car park and boatyard

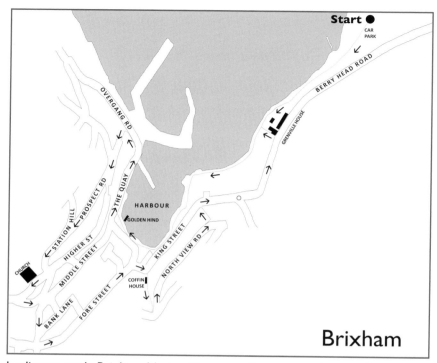

Brixham

leading towards Brixham Marina. There is a fingerpost indicating that you are heading for the town centre and harbour, and the 'Welcome to Brixham Marina' sign is very obvious. Head for it. This becomes a pleasant walkway along the front, with the marina to your right and views across the harbour. You pass Grenville House on the left and some small, pretty gardens.

> **Grenville House** dates from 1863 and was founded by the 'British Seaman's Boys' Home' charity as an orphanage, funded by local benefactor William Gibbs. After a temporary closure in 1988 it emerged as the Nautical Venture Centre two years later before changing its name to Grenville House Outdoor Education Centre in 1995. Many Devon schools use the centre to partake in all manner of organized activities such as abseiling, caving, canoeing and climbing

Beyond the marina continue to walk around the harbour, ignoring any left turns. You reach the William of Orange statue (he usually has a disrespectful seagull on his head) and beyond him a replica of the Golden Hind. Walk between the Old Market House Restaurant and the Golden Hind and continue right round the harbour until, just before the road bends left in front of the modern fish market building, you will see some steps on the left leading up from the pavement. Go up here.

William of Orange: *On 5th November 1688 Dutchman, William of Orange, landed in Brixham from where he would march to London to overthrow the catholic James II on 11th April 1689. To rub salt into the wound he subsequently married the deposed king's daughter, Mary. William of Orange became King William III and ruled alongside Mary as his queen. The statue on Brixham harbourside was erected in 1889 at a cost of £700*

The Golden Hind *is a full-size replica of Sir Francis Drake's most famous ship, in which he became the first Englishman to circumnavigate the globe. During the voyage the ship contained a crew of 80 sailors and 10 officers. The replica has been a feature in Brixham harbour since 1964, though the one seen today is a second version. The first sunk in rough seas in 1987 whilst being towed to Dartmouth to have a new keel fitted*

The first flight of steps is followed by a few single steps up a gentler gradient. There are lovely cottages on the left here. Just beyond No.14 a path goes ahead down to the road. Ignore this and instead, by No.15, go up another 2 flights of

The Golden Hind

steps. At the top the road continues ahead with more steps to the right. Ignore these steps and follow the road in front of you, this is called Overgang.

After No.33 you reach a road junction with a fork ahead. Take the right hand fork along the well-named Prospect Road. You will soon be passing the pastel-coloured cottages which you saw earlier from the harbour, it's like walking through a bag of sugared almonds. Behind and left are more good views across town and harbour. Prospect Road leads to Station Hill. You can see the church, head for this. The road bends left to a T-junction. Turn right along Church Street.

You pass the entrance to All Saints Church but at the time of our visit it was firmly locked against intruders. Continue down Church Street and about 20m further there is a sharp left turn to go down Church Hill West. Take this, and at its junction with Church Hill East turn right for a few metres to meet the main road. Here turn right along Middle Street which quickly bends left to become Market Street. The attractive late 19thC building which houses Brixham Theatre is ahead to the right. Cross Brewery Lane and continue to the crossroads. Glance right here to admire the façade of the theatre and its adjacent buildings then turn left along pedestrianised Fore Street.

Pass the Methodist Church on the right and at the end of the pedestrianisation turn right along King Street. Just along here you will see an intriguingly-shaped

Classic Brixham view from North View Road

Temperance Place

building on the right which, at the time of writing, houses a New Age style gift shop. This is Ye Olde Coffin House. An enticing flight of stairs leading up Temperance Place to the left of this building is your next direction.

> **Ye Olde Coffin House** *is thought to date from the early 19thC and was apparently built due to a father's aversion to his future son-in-law. When asked for his daughter's hand in marriage the father said he would rather see her in a coffin than see her wed. Hence they built the house in the distinctive shape of a coffin and the father, amazed by this effort, gave his blessing*

Savour this ascent – it's another sugared almond moment and the cottages are lovely. House moves to and from here must be tricky but worth it. Ignore North View Steps on your left and continue to follow the steps of Temperance Place to their top. Regain your breath, then turn sharp left along North View Road and follow this, with thirst-quenching views to the left.

Keep with North View Road until it forks, the road going right and a path called Queen's Steps to the left. The lighthouse at the end of the breakwater looks quite diminutive from up here. Follow Queen's Steps and as the path bends left you find her steps descending. A handy railing presents itself, hang on!

You reach the road with the 19thC Maritime Inn on your left. Unless you're planning an innings, go right, this is King Street again. Within 100m you reach a junction with a mini roundabout. Go left along Berry Head Road which bends left to bring you to the entrance to Grenville House. Just by its gate descend steps on the left towards the marina. At the bottom turn right and retrace your way back to the car park and the breakwater.

__The breakwater__ was eventually completed in 1916 following a design originally submitted by James Meadows Rendel in 1843. During the Second World War specially constructed ramps and piers were added to enable US soldiers to leave for the D-day landings. It stretches for almost half a mile into Torbay and culminates in a small but well-formed lighthouse. It was the last in the country to be powered by oil and was replaced in 1984 by an electric light

Ye Olde Coffin House

Dartmouth
Distance: 1¼ miles / 2km

Dartmouth is steeped in history and the atmosphere of things nautical. It has some of the most beautiful buildings and scenery to be found in a Devon town (in our opinion). With its plethora of tiny streets and independent shops and restaurants, Dartmouth makes for a really lovely day out. Allow time to browse. You may see steam trains on the other side of the river, running in and out of Kingswear. There are quite a few ups and downs throughout the walk, but the paths are good and it's very much worth the effort.

Start point: Mayor's Avenue Car Park, TQ6 9NF

Directions to start: Dartmouth is in South Devon, east of the A381 Totnes to Kingsbridge Road. If you end up on the Kingsbridge side of the River Dart there are two car ferries to take you across – a pleasant way to arrive

Parking: Mayor's Avenue Car Park

Public transport: Dartmouth is well-served by buses operated by Stagecoach Devon, West Dart and various other companies. Timetables available online at www.travelinesw.com. Nearest mainline stations are Paignton (5.8 miles) and Totnes (7.5 miles). Steam trains, operated by the Dartmouth Steam Railway and Riverboat Company (01803 555872), run from Paignton to Kingswear with a ferry across the river. Alternatively travel by boat down the River Dart from Totnes.

Refreshments: Café Alf Resco, Lower Street, 01803 835880; The Resnova Floating Inn (permanently moored on the River Dart), 07770 628967

Toilets: Adjacent to the car park and gardens

Nearby places to stay: Charity House, Collaford Lane, 01803 832176; Victorian House, Vicarage Lane, 01803 832766

Places of interest: Coleton Fishacre Gardens (NT), near Kingswear, 01803 752466; Dartmouth Castle (EH), Castle Road, 01803 833588

Market days: Tuesday and Friday

Authors' tip: If you have time and don't mind the cost, the 'round robin' trip available through Dartmouth Steam Railway and Riverboat Company (see above) is a real treat and a delightful way to explore the wider area by boat, steam train and bus

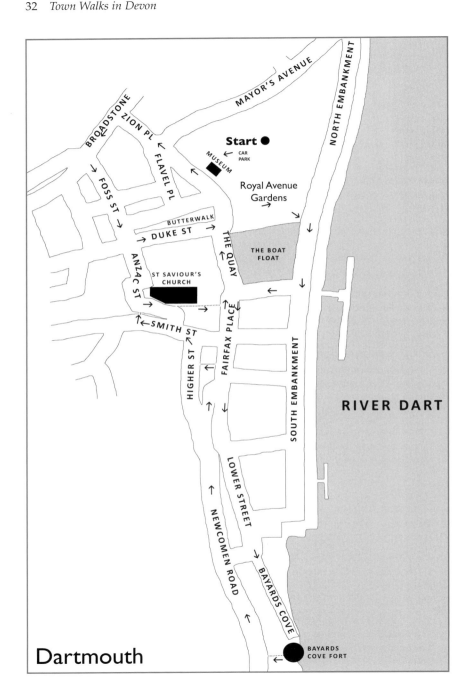

Start ●

CAR PARK

MAYOR'S AVENUE

BROADSTONE

ZION PL

FLAVEL PL

FOSS ST

MUSEUM

Royal Avenue Gardens →

NORTH EMBANKMENT

BUTTERWALK

→ DUKE ST →

THE QUAY

THE BOAT FLOAT

ANZAC ST

ST SAVIOUR'S CHURCH

← SMITH ST

FAIRFAX PLACE

HIGHER ST

SOUTH EMBANKMENT

RIVER DART

LOWER STREET

NEWCOMEN ROAD

BAYARDS COVE

BAYARDS COVE FORT

Dartmouth

Leave the car park in the corner near the TIC and the Newcomen Engine House. (You can go through the TIC to visit the engine if you wish.) Turn right along Mayor's Avenue and as the road bends right cross over, with care, and keep ahead to follow a narrow road, Zion Place, which leads off the bend. Turn left as Zion Place bends and soon the road opens up into a wider area. Go left here along the narrow and attractive Foss Street. You are heading towards the church.

> **Thomas Newcomen** *(1663–1729), an ironmonger born in Dartmouth, contributed significantly to the Industrial Revolution by inventing the first atmospheric steam engine. These were used extensively throughout Britain and Europe to pump water out of mines. The massive machine on display in Dartmouth today was used by the Coventry Canal Company*

Pass the celebrated Simon Drew gallery on your right and browse your way along. At the end of Foss Street, when you reach a small crossroads, go left along Duke Street and soon you see the remarkable Butterwalk on your left. Stand back and admire all its levels.

> **The Butterwalk:** *These beautiful, Grade I listed buildings date back to the first half of the 17thC and were built as Merchants' Houses on land reclaimed*

The Butterwalk

The Cherub

from the river. They are considered to be some of the finest examples of their type in England. Charles II held court in the end premises, now the Museum. Although damaged by bombs in 1943 repairs were carried out in the 1950s. The corbels supporting the first floor window are not all of the same date. The second from the left was carved by John Glanville over 60 years ago as his 'apprentice piece'. He still lives locally. The Butterwalk originally had 13 granite columns but now there are only 11

At the end of Duke Street cross the road to enter the Royal Avenue Gardens through their ornate wrought iron arch. A fountain with a bandstand beyond are ahead of you, with the gardens to your left. Take time to stroll around these, they aren't extensive and in summer are quite tropical. When you've had your fill return to the bandstand and leave the gardens on the opposite side to where you entered them. The River Dart is on the other side of the road.

Turn right along the road and you will see the square Boat Float on your right – a picturesque place when the tide is in. Don't drop off the edge. Keep ahead to the corner, where The Quay goes off to the right and the spectacular façade of the 19thC York House looks down at you.

The walk turns right along The Quay but it's worth first crossing the road towards the river to get a good look at the elegant buildings with their

The Boat Float

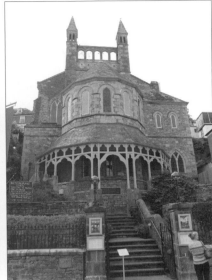

Tudor building on Fairfax Place   *St. Barnabas Church*

decorative façades facing the water along South Embankment. Across the river you can see the village of Kingswear through a cat's cradle of boat masts. Also by the river you will see Station Restaurant, no train has ever stopped here.

Dartmouth Station: *In the 1860s, when the Dartmouth and Torbay Railway first planned its route, the intention was to bring the railway over the river by bridge. There was much opposition to this idea and in the end the line went to Kingswear and passengers were ferried over to Dartmouth Station. Dartmouth Station had been built ahead of the railway so the buildings have never been used for their intended purpose. A Heritage Line still runs steam trains in and out of Kingswear*

Return to the corner by York House and walk along The Quay with the Boat Float to your right and buildings to the left. At the end turn left onto Fairfax Place, noticing on the corner the lovely half timbered, Grade II* listed building dating from 1664. On Fairfax Place look up at its first floor level and above – there are some amazing angles here! The adjacent former merchant's house on Fairfax Place is also remarkable – see the coats of arms of local notables between 1349 and 1775, and in the frieze below the first floor windows the words 'stamp office'. This house is late 16th/early 17thC.

Bayards Cove

Continue down Fairfax Place and look at the more 'modern' houses on the right hand side. Just as beautiful as their older near neighbours, these were built to replace much older buildings after the road was widened in the late 19thC. Further on, at the time of writing, a massive rebuilding project was underway, restoring the Tudor buildings destroyed by fire in May 2010.

Just before the end of Fairfax Place look right up the narrow alleyway of Horn Hill. Remember this spot as you will be back here later. Continue to the end of Fairfax Place and at the junction ahead take the left fork down Lower Street. Ignore any lefts or rights and this will take you to Bayards Cove.

A delightful spot! Loaf awhile on the benches, taking in the view downriver to Dartmouth Castle on the right bank. This area feels very venerable. Continue along the cobbled walkway beside Bayards Cove, looking out for the barometer attached to the wall of one of the houses which was presented to the mariners of Dartmouth in 1860. When you reach the fort pass under the arch, feeling the weight of centuries over your head. Bear right across the courtyard beyond, heading for the last-but-one arch in the far wall. Duck under here and beyond you will find some steps leading up to the right.

Bayards Cove *exudes oldness and this sense of authenticity made it an ideal location for the television series* The Onedin Line. *The Mayflower and The Speedwell moored here in August 1620 before setting off with the Pilgrim*

Fathers for America. The Speedwell turned back to Plymouth but the Mayflower succeeded in making the crossing. The Tudor artillery fort at the far end is now managed by English Heritage

At the top you will see steps in front leading back down and an access on the left onto Newcomen Street. Take the latter and turn right along the road. There is a good view from here across to Dartmouth Naval College on the hillside beyond and seaside-coloured houses on your left. Also on your left is the grand building of the old St. Barnabas Church. Keep heading down Newcomen Street passing the lovely St. John the Baptist Catholic Church on the left which is also worth popping in to visit. When the road forks, keep right along Newcomen Street, noticing the blue plaque which indicates that this was the site of the Guildhall until 1864. It existed here for 400 years.

St. Barnabas Church *was built in the mid 19thC but had ceased to function as a church by 1980. This grand, Grade II listed building now has a new lease of life, functioning as the Dartmouth Apprentice Restaurant*

At the junction with Lower Street and Fairfax Place keep ahead to retrace your steps for a short distance along Fairfax Place to Horn Hill which we noticed

St. Saviours as seen from Anzac Street

Fan vaulting on rood screen at St. Saviour's

earlier. Turn left up here and pause at the top of the steps. The fabulous Cherub Inn dates from around 1380 and is one of Dartmouth's oldest buildings. Tear yourself away, turning right along Higher Street until you meet Smith Street at a T-junction. Turn left, you will see The Seven Stars, which claims to be Dartmouth's oldest pub. Continue up Smith Street until, in about 50m, you find some steps on the right going down. Look out for the notice at the top of these steps: if you see anyone wheeling a barrow down them you could earn yourself five shillings. Descend these steps and at the bottom turn right, passing Town Cottage which, in 1750, was part of Dartmouth's Jail. It looks far too appealing! Continue on to visit the church of St. Saviour.

St. Saviour's Church *was founded in 1286 but not completed and consecrated until the following century. A Grade I listed building, this lovely church contains some architectural gems. It has beautiful carving in its 15thC rood screen and the timber of the 17thC gallery came from a ship captured from the Spanish Armada of 1588. Notice the mighty and elaborately carved door. Possibly the original door, carbon dating has shown that it is older than the date inscribed on it (1631) would suggest, this being the date repairs were carried out*

Emerge from the church porch and turn left. Follow the churchyard wall on the left and enter a passageway between the wall and the Seven Stars. Keep ahead along here and this leads back to Fairfax Place. Turn left and walk back to The Quay, you will see the Boat Float again over on the right. Cross the road and beyond the Boat Float you pass the entrance to the Royal Avenue Gardens on the right. Keep straight on and you will reach the TIC and car park from which you started.

Totnes
Distance: 1¾ miles / 2.8km

Totnes was first established in Saxon times although less-substantiated and older legend associates it with the arrival in Britain of Brutus of Troy, who was supposed to have landed here on arrival in England. The stone upon which he reputedly trod his first is in Fore Street, rather too high to be near the mooring for a ship, but it makes a good story. The town is a real architectural treat, saturated with listed buildings many of which house some very appealing restaurants and shops. The town is an interesting juxtaposition of traditional and 'new age' and for those of you familiar with Somerset, it's like being in Glastonbury and Wells both at the same time. The walk does comprise some uphill stretches.

Start point: Old Totnes Bridge, TQ9 5YS

Directions to start: Totnes is situated in the South Hams area of South Devon at the head of the River Dart Estuary. It is approximately 26 miles south west of Exeter. The A381 and A385 run through the town

Parking: Plenty of pay & display car parks in the town. The one on Steamer Quay Road is convenient for the start of the walk

Public transport: Totnes has an excellent bus service from many surrounding towns. Bus operators are Stagecoach Devon, Country Bus First South Devon & Tally Ho! Timetables available online at www.travelinesw.com. Totnes Railway Station is located on Station Road. Dartmouth Steam Railway and Riverboat Company (01803 555872) run an excellent riverboat service along the River Dart (see authors' tip below)

Refreshments: Greys Dining Room, 96 High Street, 01803 866369; Waterside Bistro, The Plains, 01803 864069

Toilets: Underneath the Civic Hall steps in the market place, Coronation Road (opposite the TIC) and Steamer Quay car park

Nearby places to stay: Four Seasons Guest House, 13 Bridgetown, 01803 862146; The Great Grubb B&B, Fallowfields, Plymouth Road, 01803 849071

Places of interest: Sharpham Vineyard, Ashprington, 01803 732203; Totnes Castle (EH), Castle Street, 01803 864406; Totnes Elizabethan House Museum, 70 Fore Street, 01803 863821

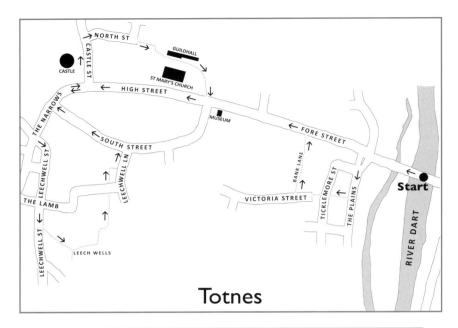

Totnes

Market days: Friday and Saturday

Authors' tip: If time allows we highly recommend the riverboat trip from Totnes to Dartmouth. This 1¼ hour cruise sets off from Steamer Quay and winds its way along this stretch of the Dart, undoubtedly one of the most scenic stretches of river in the UK

Start on the old Totnes Bridge across the River Dart, you will see the Royal Seven Stars Hotel nearby so you know you're on the right bridge. Rising above the town there is a good view of the church and castle. From the bridge, walk towards the town centre and at the broad junction with The Plains, go left, noticing in the middle of the road the memorial to William John Wills, son of Totnes and explorer of the Australian continent.

> **The bridge** *spanning the River Dart dates from 1828 and was designed by Devon architect Charles Fowler, who also designed the old Covent Garden and Hungerford Markets in London as well as the Tavistock Corn Market. Earlier bridges existed, first constructed of wood then, from around the 13thC, of stone*

Walk along The Plains for about 100m to where you find an ornate fountain on the right, commemorating the diamond jubilee of Queen Victoria. Go right here away from The Plains and follow the narrow path up the side of the Dartmouth

Inn. Cross over Ticklemore Street and continue ahead along Victoria Street. About 50m further on you will find Bank Lane on the right. Take this, it gets narrower and becomes enclosed, then emerges beside the 18thC Gothic House. Beyond here you reach Fore Street, turn left and savour the buildings as you climb. Soon you find the East Gate spanning the road.

> **Totnes Museum** *is worthy of note, not only for its collection but also for the beautiful Tudor building which houses it. Built in 1575 for the Kelland family, this is a fine example of a well-preserved, half-timbered merchant's house. It is Grade I listed*

> **The East Gate:** *Destroyed by fire in 1990, the East Gate has been painstakingly reconstructed to resemble its predecessor and is an iconic sight in Totnes. It was originally constructed when Totnes became a walled town, with alterations being carried out to the gate over the centuries. The archway was widened in 1835. The line of the medieval town walls is now partly followed by North Street and the Ramparts Walk, later in this walk*

Beyond the East Gate continue uphill along High Street, passing St. Mary's Church on the right. From here look back down to the East Gate, it's a good angle from

The Gothic House

East Gate

which to view it, you can see right through the windows of the clock room. Continue up High Street, passing Market Square on the left after which the road begins to narrow with colonnaded ambulatories on both sides of the road, The Butterwalk on the right and The Poultry Walk on the left.

The Butterwalk and The Poultry Walk *are covered paths which were built to protect the produce once sold in the markets on these sites*

Continue with High Street as it bends left, this area is known as The Narrows. Pass South Street on the left and the next left is Leechwell Street. Take this (although if you are visiting Greys Dining Rooms, which we do recommend, you will need to go a little further along High Street to find it.) Leechwell Street widens, continue ahead crossing a road called The Lamb (you will see a cottage called Lamb Corner on the right), and keep directly on until you reach the Kingsbridge Inn. Just in front of its entrance, on the left, a little path leads to the Leech Wells. Follow this.

The Leech Wells *were reputedly a source of healing water. Lepers from a hospital just outside Totnes were said to frequent the springs in the hope of restoring health, although it seems unlikely that this would have been permitted.*

The Poultry Walk

Generally the water was thought to be curative for skin and eye conditions. The three troughs collecting the water are clearly visible and were once named Toad, Long Crippler (a slow worm) and Snake. This area is also a junction of three footpaths and behind one of the enclosing walls is a triangular immersion pool, evidence of the importance of 'trinities' in some beliefs. The springs were so well-used in the Middle Ages that they were placed under the care of town wardens

At a T-junction you find the wells situated on the right, Leechwell Cottage is ahead. Go left along a narrow, walled path and follow it as it winds along to emerge at a crossing road. Cross, and re-enter the path opposite which soon bends right to reach Leechwell Lane. Turn left and at the T-junction with South Street go left again, uphill. There are public loos in the area to your right as you ascend here and look roof-wards for a view of enormous pottery cockerels on a house which was once occupied by a potter. South Street leads you back to The Narrows.

Turn right and return along the High Street until you reach the next turning on the left. This is Castle Street. Take this and within 100m you see a path on the left leading up to Totnes Castle, managed by English Heritage. There is an attractive view of North Gate ahead of you. From the footpath to the castle the walk continues by crossing Castle Street and heading along North Street.

Totnes Castle: *A typical motte and bailey castle was built here after the Norman Conquest, dominating the earlier Saxon town. Stone fortifications were constructed during medieval times. A hall and domestic buildings would once have been within the enclosure but no longer survive. The castle has had a succession of owners down the centuries*

Keep ahead along North Street and as the road bends left continue straight on along a narrow path which bends about to soon reach the church. Follow the path behind the church with Guildhall Cottage on the left and within a few metres you emerge at the startlingly old Guildhall. Pass the first gate on the right into the churchyard and continue along Guildhall Yard until you reach a second gateway leading to the churchyard. Enter here to explore and to visit this elegant 15thC building.

The Guildhall: *The Grade I listed Guildhall is on the site of an 11thC Benedictine Priory and possibly some of its foundations date from this time. It has a colourful history. In the 16thC Edward VI gave the town a charter which permitted the building to be re-employed as a school and guildhall and this is* *when it mostly dates from. During its life it has also been used as a gaol, magistrate's court and council chambers. The town council still meets here*

St. Mary's Church *dates from 1450 although there has been a church on the site since earlier times. Go inside to see the graceful rood screen with its lovely stone tracery and the oak 'wagon roof'. Prior to the Dissolution of the Monasteries in the 16thC a priory church abutted this parish church building*

Leave the church and return to the gate by which you entered, passing through an avenue of memorial medlar trees. Turn right to continue along the path, this is The Ramparts Walk. The cottages on your left are larger than they appear from this vantage point, as this path passes at their roof level. Descend the steps to arrive back under East Gate. Here turn left down Fore Street and look out for The Brutus Stone, set into the pavement about 90m along on the left – there is a marker on the adjacent wall to help you spot it. Keep going down hill, passing Bank Lane on the right and continuing ahead to the bridge from whence you started.

St. Mary's Church tower   Brutus Stone

Salcombe
Distance: 2½ miles / 4km

This is a walk of contrasts. Unusually, for a town walk, it follows a delightful woodland path in the early stages. Bear in mind that this will require you to be wearing flat shoes so leave the stilettos behind today. It is quite steep in places as Salcombe, like many towns on coast and estuary, is built up the cliff. The walk takes you through an elegant residential area before dropping back down to the bustle of little streets in the centre. Salcombe has quite a tropical feel in summer, enhanced by blue skies and exotic trees and plants. If you're not there on a blue-sky day you must take our word for this. We've spent much time here over the years, it's appealing in all weathers and if you're here during Salcombe Regatta there is a wonderful air of festival.

Start point: North Sands Car Park, TQ8 8LD

Directions to start: Salcombe is located in the South Hams area of South Devon on the west side of the Salcombe Estuary. It is approximately 25 miles south east of Plymouth and can be approached via the A379 or the A381

Parking: North Sands Car Park (pay & display)

Public transport: Salcombe is linked by buses to the following towns: Kingsbridge, Totnes, Exeter, Newton Abbot. Bus operators are Tally Ho! and Stagecoach Devon. Timetables available at www.travelinesw.com. The closest railway stations are Ivybridge (12.3 miles) and Totnes (14.2 miles)

Refreshments: Captain Flint's, 82 Fore Street, 01548 842357; The Winking Prawn Beach Café & BBQ, North Sands, 01548 842326

Toilets: North Sands and Whitestrand Car Park

Nearby places to stay: Meadow View, 11 Longfield Drive, 01548 844102; Threshold, 20a Longfield Drive, 01548 842877

Places of interest: Overbeck's (NT), Sharpitor, 01548 842893; Salcombe Maritime and Local History Museum, Market Street, 01548 843726

Market days: None

Authors' tip: If the weather is sunny, and time allows, consider taking the ferry across to East Portlemouth. From here a walk southwards along the estuary will reveal a collection of lovely sandy coves. Alternatively

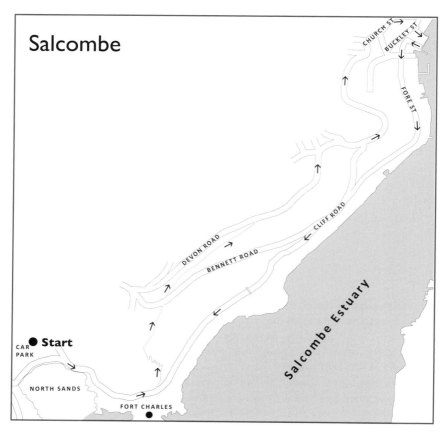

Salcombe

you could flop with a coffee at the waterside Venus Café (situated close to the ferry pontoon) whilst enjoying the boating activity and splendid views

From the car park cross the road and admire the view across the bay. This is North Sands. Turn left along the pavement with the sea to your right. You start to climb and pass the public loos on the left. Keep climbing and soon you will see, over the wall on the right and close to the water's edge, the ruins of Fort Charles. Continue beyond these and as the road flattens out and begins to descend you will see a public footpath going left off the road. Take this.

Fort Charles (Salcombe Castle) was built during the reign of Henry VIII to defend the estuary against pirates. It became a busy place during the English

Civil War when Edmund Fortescue rebuilt it as a royalist stronghold in 1643. He named it Fort Charles in honour of the king. It was under siege from January to May 1646 and was the last place in the war to surrender to the Parliamentarian troops. It was then deliberately ruined by order of Parliament

The path zigzags upwards, as you climb you will be rewarded with glimpses to the right across the estuary (although this body of water is technically a 'ria' – an estuary with no major river running into it). East Portlemouth and its idyllic beaches are on the opposite side. You reach Bennett Road (although there is no sign). Cross over, bearing right, and about 10m away you find access to another ascending footpath. The path is to the right of steps leading into a private garden – make sure you get the path and not the garden. This leads up through a Woodland Trust area called The Plantation. You reach steps which bring you out onto Devon Road where you will find view-rich benches, should you need them.

From the top of the steps turn right along Devon Road and keep following it as it continues to descend and bend after the junction with Herbert Road, this is signposted for Town Centre. You will pass some rather gracious houses along this stretch and eventually the red brick Catholic Church on the left. Lovely views across the estuary are frequent and soon after the Catholic Church Devon

Fort Charles   Memorial

Road bends again and you will see Holy Trinity Church ahead of you, watching over the town.

Devon Road ends at a junction with Onslow Road (again there is no sign) but if you bear right you are still heading for the church which helps to guide you. This is Holy Trinity Church and is open to visitors.

Holy Trinity Church *is comparatively modern. Built in 1843, it contains artefacts from older churches including a medieval water stoop. Enjoy its light and airy interior. If you're lucky, as we were, you'll be treated to the rich sound of organ practise*

Leave the church, turning left out of the gate and go down Church Street, ignoring Market Street to the right. The wall of the church grounds is on the left. Church Street bends right, bend with it and this leads to a V-junction. Turn right here, admiring picturesque Buckley Street ahead of you. Within a very few metres you will see steps on the left leading down. Take these, they bring you out between cottages and thence to a walkway beside the waterfront with railings to stop you dropping over the edge. Turn right here and immediately left, following the walkway beside the water. It then bends right. Keep on, with the

Holy Trinity Church

Fabulous estuary views can be seen on much of this walk

water to your left, and soon you reach the RNLI station. Turn right at the RNLI to follow Union Street which turns left at the 18thC Fortescue Inn, into Fore Street.

At the small crossroads you will see the Maritime Museum and TIC along the road on the right, but the walk continues ahead along Fore Street. Explore its nooks, crannies and lovely, individual shops....but generally keep straight on along Fore Street which eventually becomes Cliff Road.

You will pass a memorial garden to your left with a monument to those who died in the Two World Wars and also in the Salcombe Lifeboat Disaster. Beyond the memorial continue along Cliff Road with its fine buildings. This is easy walking but look out for traffic. When you reach the junction with Bennett Road fork left. You have good estuary views to the left. The road passes under a little stone bridge and you will eventually see the ruins of Fort Charles again on your left. Beyond North Sands is the more distant beach of South Sands with its lovely wooded backdrop, which was reputedly considered by the Prince Regent, later George IV, as a site for his pavilion. He ultimately plumped for Brighton. Continue and you will find yourself back at the start point.

Salcombe Lifeboat Disaster *of 27 October 1916 was a tragedy that didn't need to happen. The lifeboat, the William and Emma, reached the stricken schooner, Western Lass, only to find that her crew had already been rescued. Of the 15 lifeboat crew 13 died leaving widows and 12 small children. One of the two survivors, Edwin Distin became the coxwain of the next lifeboat. The seas around Salcombe have always been perilous for shipping. In 2009 the remains of a* ***Bronze Age ship*** *were discovered, dating from roughly 1000BC. The ship was just 300m from shore and was importing ingots of copper and tin from mainland Europe*

Fore Street offers a pleasurable browse

Walk 7
Exeter
Distance: 2¾ miles / 4.5km

Although Exeter, the county town of Devon, suffered extensive damage during WWII many architectural gems remain, often juxtaposed with very contrasting modern buildings. This mixture of styles in no way detracts from the attractiveness of the area. The walk takes in some of the verdant green oases of the city, of which there are quite a number, as well as a wealth of ancient buildings and historic sites. The majority of the walk is on paths and pavements but the stretch around the catacombs is on grass. This is a short 'there-and-back-again' section so can be missed out by those wishing to keep tarmac under their soles and also by those not wishing to visit an historic, but possibly rather eerie, cemetery.

Start point: Southernhay Church on the corner of Dix's Field and Southernhay East

Directions to start: Exeter is situated slightly to the east of the county and can be accessed from both the M5 and A30

Parking: Many options – The Civic Centre or Princesshay Car Parks on Dix's Field are the closest to the start

Public transport: Exeter is well-served by buses from surrounding towns with the Paris Street Bus & Coach Station conveniently located just 200m from the start of this walk. Timetables available online at www.travelinesw.com. The city has two central, mainline stations: Exeter St. David's and Exeter Central

Refreshments: Cathedral Café, Exeter Cathedral, 01392 285988; Herbies (vegetarian), 15 North Street, 01392 258473; No. 21, 21 Cathedral Yard, 01392 210303

Toilets: Catherine Square and Paris Street Bus Station

Nearby places to stay: Number Twelve, 12 Queens Terrace, 01392 213079; Raffles, 11 Blackall Road, 01392 270200; Woodbine Guesthouse, 1 Woodbine Terrace, 01392 203302

Places of interest: Exeter Cathedral, Cathedral Green, 01392 285983; Exeter Guildhall, High Street, 01392 265524; Exeter's Underground Passages, 2 Paris Street, 01392 665887; Quay House Visitor Centre, 46 The Quay, 01392 271611; Royal Albert Memorial Museum & Art Gallery, Queen Street, 01392 665 858; St. Nicholas Priory, The Mint, Off Fore Street, 01392 421252; Tuckers Hall, Fore Street, 01392 412348

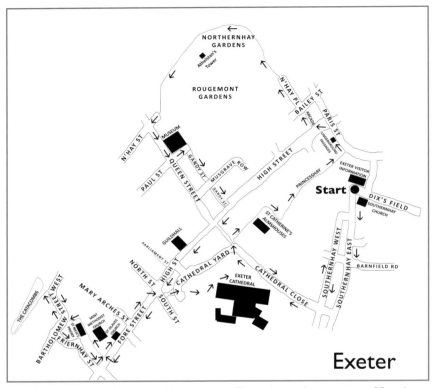

Exeter

Market days: Farmers' Market every Thursday at the junction of South Street and Fore Street, 9am–2pm. Every Sunday there is a general market and car boot sale at 6.45am–12.45pm. This takes place at the Matford Park and Ride Car Park at Matford Park Road, Marsh Barton

Authors' tip: If time allows we recommend an excursion to Exeter's Historic Quayside which is approximately a ½ mile walk from the Cathedral. Try to ensure your route takes you past the impressive timber-framed 'The House That Moved' at the corner of West Street and Frog Street. Look out for the medieval bridge near the Exe Bridges roundabout

From Southernhay Church walk along Southernhay East. You pass attractive Georgian buildings on the left with the central, leafy gardens which divide Southernhay East from Southernhay West on your right. At the junction with Barnfield Road turn right to cross through the central gardens, then left to continue in the same direction as before along Southernhay West, with the elegant façades on your right and the gardens to the left.

Southernhay, *now one of Exeter's public gardens, runs along the line of the old town defense ditch, the Crulditch, which was just outside the Roman city walls. Excavations indicate even earlier occupation of the site, with Iron Age remains being discovered in 2002. The architecture now is predominantly Georgian although more modern buildings comfortably fill the gaps left by WWII bombs. There have been gardens here since the 17thC. The area is reputedly haunted by a black pig*

At the end of the terrace you find a right turn into Cathedral Close which passes through the Roman city walls and into the area of the Cathedral. Take this right turn, passing under an attractive wrought iron bridge with glimpses of the Cathedral over the wall to your left. The area opens out to give views across the green – there are architectural delights in every direction. Continue towards the buildings of the Royal Clarence Hotel. When you reach it glance ahead up the narrow and enticing Martin's Lane and also notice on your right the ancient St. Martin's Church, the oldest part of which pre-dates the Norman Conquest.

Cathedral Close: *This beautiful area was once the main burial site for Exeter. It has been estimated that half a million bodies were buried here. The attractive buildings around The Close, several of which are Grade 1 listed, now serve a variety of purposes including as restaurants and residences for the*

Cathedral Close

clergy. The Devonshire Association 'for the Advancement of Science, Literature and the Arts' also has offices here

---

Exeter Cathedral: *The Saxon predecessor to our present-day cathedral was near the current building's West Front. The construction of the Norman Cathedral commenced in 1114, was completed about 1180 and was about 2/3 the length of the current building. It was then rebuilt during the Middle Ages in the Decorated style although Norman features were retained – the square towers being a prime example. During WWII many of the Cathedral treasures were removed for safety, including some of the stained glass, but the Chapel of St. James took a direct hit in 1942. The capital from one of its pillars now resides in the Cathedral Café*

Turn right here, soon passing through Catherine Square with the romantic ruins of the Almshouses on your right. Over to the left is St. Stephen's Church, continue ahead, passing St. Stephen's House, to reach the junction with Bedford Street. Turn right here for about 50m then left into the contemporary Princesshay Shopping Precinct. Glance back here – there's a lovely view of the Cathedral peering over its very modern neighbours.

Exeter Cathedral

St. Catherine's Almshouses: *The earliest reference to Almshouses in Exeter dates back to the 11thC when the St. Mary Magdalene Hospital was built. That building has gone, although the site is still used for Almshouses. St. Catherine's, which you see here, were founded in the 15thC and had tiny rooms, measuring some 6' x 5'. By the late 19thC they weren't considered to be of sufficiently high standard to continue as Almshouses. The Church Army then took them over to provide accommodation for destitute people, until the buildings were damaged during WWII. They are now preserved as a memorial to the Exeter Blitz in May 1942*

Keep ahead past the shops, passing the Blue Boy statue, who marks the site of an old Blue Coat School which was founded here in 1636. There are more remains of the city wall on your right. A short distance beyond the wall you reach the junction with Paris Street. Turn left, soon passing the entrance to the Underground Passages on your left. A little further, at the junction with High Street, cross over, bearing slightly left, to a small arcade between shops about 20m away – notice the ornate clock on the wall above its glazed roof. Turn right off the High Street down this arcade and at its end cross the road and continue ahead up Northernhay Place.

Underground Passages: *These were built during the 14thC to carry pipes which brought fresh water from the springs outside the town into Exeter. The lead pipes often leaked so to avoid the disruption of constantly digging them up they were housed in these vaulted passages. (Seven centuries later – and we dig up.) They are the only such passages in the country open to the public*

City Walls: *Exeter as a site of human habitation predates the Roman town (circa 55AD) by many centuries but it was the Romans who originally built the wonderful protective wall, much of which can still be seen. The fortified Roman settlement of Exeter was the most south westerly in Britain and the walls endured for 400 years. When the Romans left, decay set in but restoration of the walls was undertaken in the 9thC and 10thC and later during Norman and medieval times. They now remain as a striking monument to Exeter's colourful history*

Pass through the gates into pretty Northernhay Gardens, a Grade II listed open space and the oldest public open space in the country dating from 1612. Pass the Deer Stalker and bear slightly left on the broad main path. You'll now meet some historic local dignitaries as you enjoy the gardens: William Courtenay, 11th Earl of Devon, is on your left and soon you'll find Stafford Henry Northcote,

Earl of Iddesleigh on your right. Good views across Exeter open up ahead of you and you will see an obelisk on the left commemorating the founding in Devonshire of the Volunteer Force of Great Britain. A bandstand is over to the right.

Just after this look for a path on the left going uphill back on yourself and take this, following it as it bends right, ascending steps to a path which leads to Athelstan's Tower. Athelstan was a Saxon King who is recorded as having built a castle in Exeter, destroyed in 1003 by the Danes. Athelstan is much older than this tower which bears his name. Peek through the tower into the adjoining Rougemont Gardens which are there for exploration if you wish. Beyond these are the buildings of the present-day Exeter Castle with the ruins of the Norman building beyond.

Retrace your route down from Athelstan's Tower to the top of the flight of steps but don't descend them, instead follow the path left which goes down to rejoin the main path. Turn left and continue ahead past the War Memorial to the exit gates, bidding farewell to John Dinham in his tranquil gardens as you emerge onto Northernhay Gate, finding yourself back in the hubbub of the town. A short road from the gardens leads to Queen Street, turn left, passing the Royal Albert Memorial Museum, and then take the next left into the cobbled Gandy Street. After about 50m Gandy Street turns right, go with it and continue through this quaint little shopping area, crossing over at the junction with Musgrave Row and Little Queen Street and continuing until Gandy Street leads you to High Street.

Turn right here, admiring the gorgeous Tudor façades of the shops on your right. These façades are all that remain of the original buildings. Pass the other end of Martin's Lane on your left and, a little further on, Laura Ashley, whose premises once hosted Judge Jeffries during the Bloody Assizes after the Monmouth Rebellion. Continue as far as the grand entrance to the Exeter Guildhall – and if you're passing on a day when this is open to the public pop in and savour its ancientness.

The Exeter Guildhall *is one of the oldest municipal buildings in the country and is still used for council meetings. Early references to a guildhall here go back as far as the 12thC. The building we can visit today is largely late 15thC with the grand entrance porch dating from 1593. This cost just under £800, rather more expensive than the wonderful oak door of the same date, which cost £4.50. Notice the lovely timber roof structure. The chandelier is late 18thC and cost almost £29. Alterations to the building took place during the 19thC. The Guildhall can now be hired as a fabulous wedding venue*

After this continue down High Street, passing the weenie Parliament Street on your right which is a mere 25" at its narrowest point and is believed to be the narrowest street in the world. If you can fit into it be reassured about the broadness of your hips. Continue on High Street, admiring the oldness of St. Petrock's Church on your left. Cross over the junction with North and South Streets and keep straight on downhill (this is now Fore Street) crossing Mary Arches Street and noticing the lovely views across the Exe Valley ahead of you. Pass the venerable St. Olave's Church on your right followed by the younger Mint Methodist Church. Just after this look out for the narrow entrance on the right into the alley known as The Mint, and take this.

You'll find some lovely enclosed gardens down here together with the very old St. Nicholas Priory. Beyond this The Mint bears left and emerges on Bartholomew Street. Ahead of you is a churchyard with some lovely mature trees, although the church was demolished in the mid 20thC. Leave The Mint and walk ahead, with the churchyard to your left. The road bends right in about 70m and ahead you see the spire of St. Michael's Church. At the bend keep ahead and pass through the gates and down steps to enter the area of the catacombs. Turn left along the path which soon becomes grassy, you are above the catacombs here with the park-like St. Bartholomew's Cemetery down to the

The Guildhall

The narrowest street in the world

right and St. Michael's Church in the modern 'Georgian' Dinham Crescent beyond. Keep on the path as it descends to turn sharply right back on itself, passing through the cemetery until, in about 100m, you find a flight of steps on your right leading up to the entrance to the catacombs. Ascend these, peer through the grilled gates and ponder.....

St. Nicholas Priory is the guest wing of a former Benedictine monastery dating back to the late 11thC. It was built by the monks who were responsible for nearby St. Olave's Church. Much of their monastery was destroyed during the reign of Henry VIII but during the late 16thC the remnants of the building which we see today were occupied by a family named Hurst. It is as a town house of the well-to-do that the Priory is now presented and is open to the public on certain days of the week

Catacombs: Exeter's increasing population during the 19thC necessitated the provision of extra burial space outside the city walls. St. Bartholomew's Cemetery and its catacombs were built in the mid 1830s at great expense and were designed to appeal to the wealthy who didn't wish their mortal remains to be at risk from grave robbers. These catacombs are built in an Egyptian style and the bodies within are contained in rows, one above the other in sealed cell-like structures slightly larger than the coffins. A corridor runs along the rows and a wall divides the Anglican occupants from the non-conformist. Their capacity would have been over 2,000 bodies but less than 20 people availed themselves of the opportunity to be immured in the catacombs. During the swine flu scare of 2009 there was some thought that, if Exeter succumbed in a pandemic, these catacombs might be brought back into temporary use. Red Coat guided tours are available to visit the catacombs

Leave the catacombs and make your way back up to the gate onto Bartholomew Street. Retrace your steps towards The Mint, pass it and bear right on Bartholomew Street West until, in about 50m, you turn left into a narrow road. This is Friernhay Street. Follow it as it bends round, passing the other side of St. Nicholas Priory's gardens. Soon you emerge back onto Fore Street. Turn left and retrace your steps back to the junction with South Street (just before St. Petrock's Church) and turn right along South Street for a brief 10m, before turning left through a broad opening into Cathedral Yard again. This offers a superb view of the West Front of the Cathedral and the opportunity to savour this beautiful area again. Notice the attractive gabled shop fronts on your right. The walk crosses The Green back to Cathedral Close through which you wandered earlier. Turn right to retrace your steps along The Close and back to Southernhay.

Gandy Street

St. Catherine's Chapel and Almshouses

Old façades on High Street

Walk 8
Colyton
Distance: 1 mile / 1.6km

This delightful, friendly town provides a short, easy walk with some fascinating history and lovely Beer stone buildings. Colyton was regarded, during the Monmouth Rebellion of 1685, as being the most insurgent town in Devon. One hundred and five men from Colyton – more than from any other Devon town – went to fight for the Protestant Duke of Monmouth in his struggle against Catholic James ll. The walk follows good paths and is pretty level throughout.

Start point: Dolphin Street Car Park, EX24 6NA

Directions to start: Colyton is located in East Devon and can be accessed via the A3052 at Colyford

Parking: Dolphin Street Car Park (pay & display)

Public transport: Colyton is served by buses from many local towns. These are operated by Stagecoach South West, Axe Valley Mini-Travel and First Dorset. Timetables available online at www.travelinesw.com. Nearest railway stations are at: Axminster (4 miles) and Honiton (6½ miles). And, of course, there is the Seaton Tramway – a most pleasurable way to travel between Colyton and Seaton

Refreshments: The Cobblers Restaurant, Dolphin Street, 01297 552825; The Gerrard Arms, Rosemary Lane, 01297 552588

Toilets: Dolphin Street Car Park

Nearby places to stay: Combe House B&B, Queen Street, 01297 552640; The Old Bakehouse B&B, Lower Church Street, 01297 552518

Places of interest: Beer Quarry Caves, Quarry Lane, Beer, 01297 680282; Seaton Tramway, Colyton Station House, Station Road, 01297 552717; Shute Barton (NT), Shute, 01752 346585

Market days: At the time of writing the market had ceased for the foreseeable future

Authors' tip: Don't leave this area before taking a trip on the Seaton Tramway. This lovely 3-mile route leaves Colyton to pass through the bird-rich Axe Valley en route to the seaside town of Seaton

Leave the car park and turn right along Dolphin Street, passing the public garden on your left. Take the next turning left onto Lower Church Street with its pretty

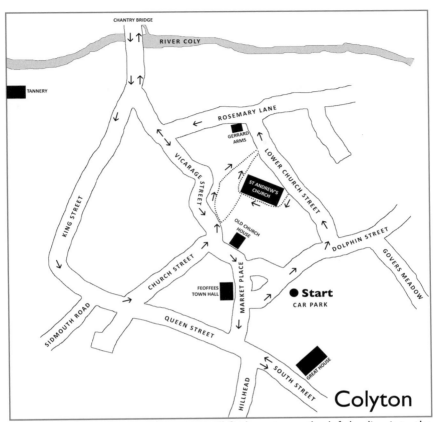

Colyton

cottages. A short distance along you will find a gate on the left leading into the churchyard. Enter here to explore the glorious church with its octagonal lantern tower.

> **St. Andrew's Church** *is a bright and airy delight. Steeped in history, look out for the Courtenay Monument. This is a memorial to Margaret Beaufort, Countess of Devon, who was the granddaughter of John of Gaunt and Katherine Swynford (the eponymous heroine of Anya Seton's famous novel, Katherine). The church's west window is of cathedral-proportions, one of the largest found in any parish church. There is also a rather splendid cockerel on the weather vane. He is 1.4m long, 0.9m high and weighs 32kg (70lb)*

After visiting the church turn right out of the porch and follow the path round the building to a gate which leads back onto Lower Church Street, a little further on from the point at which you left it earlier. Turn left and on your left you will find the Gerrard Arms. This is on the junction with Rosemary Lane.

> **Gerrard Arms:** *This old coaching inn dates back to 1506 when it would have had stabling to accommodate changes of horses for passing coaches. A fire in 1914 destroyed its thatch. Lawrence of Arabia is said to have visited*

Turn left along Rosemary Lane and at the end you will face the grand gates of Colyton House, an 18thC Grade II listed building. Turn right here along Vicarage Street to the end of the road. At the corner with Chantry Cottage turn right along King Street to Chantry Bridge spanning the River Coly. There is an enticing footpath beside the river if you are booted and wish to explore. The name 'Coly' derives from the old English 'culli' meaning 'narrow'.

Our walk now retraces back along King Street, passing Rosemary Lane on the left followed by the entrance drive to the historic tannery on your right. Continue along King Street as it bends left with the Methodist Church on the right. After this you pass more attractive houses on the left, one with a memorial plaque to the men who died in the Monmouth Rebellion.

> **Tannery:** *There has been a leather tannery here for centuries and this is now the only oak bark tannery still using this traditional method in Britain. The present tannery buildings date from the early 19thC with the Trade Directory of 1830 mentioning a "tannery on a very extensive scale"*

Keep ahead, passing Colyton Cottage of 1610 on your right, then take the next left along Church Street with another good view of the church tower ahead. This leads into Market Place. Cross over towards the church gate and take the little footpath to the left of the gate which skirts the churchyard, passing cottages on the left and later another public garden.

At the end of the path turn left and left again round our old friend the Gerrard Arms, and once more walk along Rosemary Lane. This time, when you reach the gates of Colyton House, go left on Vicarage Street. You pass Berry House on the left and then bend right with the road passing the gate to The Vicarage on your right. After this the road bends left and re-enters Market Place.

Walk through Market Place, noting the Old Church House on the left and Feoffees Town Hall on the right, bearing right with the road as it continues through Market Place to the junction with Queen Street and South Street. There is an ornate lantern opposite the junction. Here turn left along South Street for a short distance to find the stout entrance gate to the privately owned Great House on the left. You can just glimpse this late 16thC, Grade II* listed building over the wall.

St. Andrew's Church

Old Church House

Attractive cottages abound in Colyton

The Feoffees: *It all began when landowner, Henry Courtney, was beheaded for treason in 1539 with his lands being confiscated by King Henry VIII. A group of local merchants and farmers sent a petition to the king to buy back his Colyton estate. This request was granted and his properties and land were secured for the huge fee of 1,000 marks under a Deed of Enfeoffment. This meant that any resulting income had to be spent on the community. And so the Feoffees were born. They began by establishing a Grammar school in 1559. Subsequently they engineered a channel of fresh water into the town and conceived an early fire service. In 1920, they sold off all their land to raise money for charity and to construct a Feoffees Town Hall. Today the Feoffees are members of a registered charity that meets frequently with the town council for the benefit of the community. They still hold an annual banquet in February where the names responsible for that original purchase are read out*

Church Houses *are the medieval equivalent of the Village Hall, their main purpose having been to raise funds for the church. Often they would be venues for church ales, a celebration consisting of a sport, plays and morris dancing – all enhanced by a strong beer often brewed on the premises. With the rise of Puritanism such festivities were deemed inappropriate and church houses were closed. After 1600 the buildings began to see use as schools, poor houses or inns. The impressive part-medieval church house in Colyton was used for the grammar school from 1612 to the 1920s. It also once served as a meeting house for the Feoffees. Over 60 church houses are known to exist in Devon*

The Great House *is a private Elizabethan house situated within extensive walled gardens. It is acknowledged to have been built by John Yonge, an eminent Elizabethan 'merchant adventurer'. His son, Walter (1579–1649), wrote many of his famous diaries whilst living here. They contain valuable historical accounts of wars overseas and were later published by the Camden Society in 1848. Four volumes now reside in The British Museum. Walter's son John had the distinction of being knighted by Charles I in 1625 and subsequently made a baronet by Charles II 36 years later. As the years moved on the house continued to be passed through the family. On 30th August 1680 another Walter Yonge entertained the Duke of Monmouth at Great House. But when the rebellious Duke landed at Lyme Regis in 1685 Walter was keen to disassociate himself and, to convince loyalty to the King, a plaster relief of the Royal Coat of Arms was quickly installed in the very room where Monmouth had stayed*

From here retrace your steps back to the Market Place where you bear right down Dolphin Street back to the car park.

Sidmouth
Distance: 3¼ miles / 5.25km

Regency architecture and summer flowers blend perfectly in this most genteel and elegant of seaside towns. Sidmouth lies in a beautiful coastal valley framed by distinctive red Triassic cliffs. Famous visitors include Queen Victoria who, as a 6-month-old princess, spent Christmas 1819 here with her parents, the Duke and Duchess of Kent. During their stay her father was taken ill with pneumonia and died the following month. Years later Victoria's 3rd son, the Duke of Connaught, visited the town where his grandfather had died and gave his name to the beautiful gardens at the start of this walk. The route is fairly level aside from the descent of Jacob's Ladder – don't worry though it's actually a perfectly negotiable staircase! A gentler ascent returns you to the car park at the end.

Start point: Manor Road Long Stay Car Park, EX10 8RU

Directions to start: Sidmouth is situated on the south coast about 15 miles south east of Exeter. It can be accessed from the A3052

Parking: Manor Road Long Stay Car Park (pay & display)

Public transport: Sidmouth is served by buses from many surrounding towns. Timetables available online at www.travelinesw.com. Nearby railway stations: Feniton (7 miles), Whimple (7.4 miles), Honiton (7.8 miles)

Refreshments: Brown's, 33 Fore Street, 01395 516724; Clock Tower Café, Connaught Gardens, 01395 515319; The Pea Green Boat Café, The Esplanade, 01395 514152

Toilets: Connaught Gardens, The Esplanade (east side near River Sid) and Sidmouth Market building

Nearby places to stay: The Hollies Guest House, Salcombe Road, 01395 514580; The Longhouse, Salcombe Hill Road, 01395 577973; Salcombe Close House, Sid Lane, 01395 579067

Places of interest: Bicton Park Botanical Gardens, East Budleigh, 01395 568465; Norman Lockyer Observatory, Salcombe Hill, 01297 680209; Sidmouth Museum, Hope Cottage, Church Street, 01395 516139

Market days: A few permanent stalls in Sidmouth Market building

Authors' tip: In fine weather thrust yourself into a deckchair on the Main Lawn of Connaught Gardens and relax. You may even be treated to a concert from the bandstand

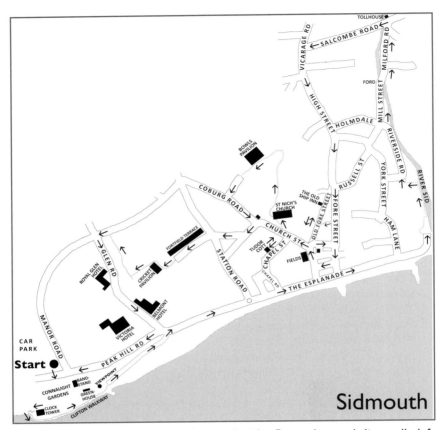

Leave the car park via steps on the south side. Cross the road diagonally left and go up the steps to Connaught Gardens. It's difficult to get lost in these beautiful gardens so self-guided exploration is recommended. Seek out the following: the Topiary Garden on the east side behind the bandstand; the Show House (greenhouse), south of the Topiary Garden, in which you'll find a range of cacti and carnivorous plants; the viewpoint just outside the garden to the east of the Show House for a spectacular view along the Jurassic Coast and over Sidmouth; the Jungle just to the west of the Show House; the Sunken Garden and Lime Kiln Garden further west. The latter comes complete with the added enticement of a pot of tea at the excellent Clock Tower Café.

Connaught Gardens *as we see them today have evolved from private gardens of the 19thC. They were bought by the local council in the 1930s, after which the dilapidated house on the site was demolished. Its gardens were* *modified and developed by the Gardens Department of Dartington Hall,Totnes. They were closed to the public during WWII when they played a role in coastal defence. Military hardware was installed and the Clock Tower had a search light fitted.This building has its origins in a 17thC lime kiln but now makes a delightful tea rooms*

Leave the Clock Tower Café tea gardens through the archway, admiring the spectacular coastal view as you do. Turn left here and go down some concrete steps, which lead you onto the wooden flight of stairs known as Jacob's Ladder. At the bottom, glance up at the cliffs to spot a cottage precariously perched on the edge. One can only ponder at the length of the lease! If you look further west on a clear day you'll also see the red sandstone rock stacks of Ladram Bay.

Jacob's Ladder: *Access to the beach from the gardens above was first established in the mid 19thC when steps and paths were cut into the cliff.This eroded away over the years and a very long ladder (hence the name) was installed. However, this was difficult to negotiate in the fashions of the day so a less-steep option was built, very like that which we use today*

From the steps turn left along the excellent Clifton Walkway.The path hugs the red Triassic rocks and if you're following these directions correctly the sea should be on your right.

Connaught Gardens

Jacob's Ladder   Clifton Walkway

Continue along the path, which soon runs along the back of the beach and then emerges onto The Esplanade by the grand edifice of the Belmont Hotel. Turn right keeping the sea on your right whilst admiring the feast of regency architecture on your left. Progress for 600m along The Esplanade until the road ends at a left bend. Here you will find public toilets on the left and a wonderful view along the coast to the right. You'll also see the River Sid on your right with Alma Bridge spanning it. This was named after the Battle of the Alma of 1854, considered to be the first battle of the Crimean War.

> **The Esplanade** *is an architectural delight, the earliest building along it dating from around 1790. Look out for the old Sidmouth Brine Baths and The Beach House, amongst many others. Blue plaques give details of the properties*

After the left bend in the road keep ahead to join the path beside the river. Stroll along this for 90m before turning left through a gap in the wall. Cross a small bridge with a playground on your left. A short distance beyond the bridge bear right through some railings, to then turn right along Riverside Road. The river is to your right with houses on the left.

After 150m this road leads to a small crossroads. Turn right here along Mill Street passing the Master's House on your left to reach a ford. Stand on the footbridge here and hope for some passing cars as it's really rather exciting to watch them splash through.

Cross the footbridge and continue in the same direction as before, but this time on the other side of the river. You are now on Milford Road with some attractive houses on the right. Continue along here for 150m to reach the Greek revival style Byes Toll House. This dates from the early 19thC and controlled the eastern approach to the town.

To the right of the tollhouse you'll see an entrance to The Byes. This is delightful, level parkland following the River Sid. Although not part of the walk it offers a tranquil stroll before returning back to the main route.

Back at Byes Toll House cross the river on the bridge and continue west towards town along Salcombe Road. After 200m you reach a T-junction faced by the Radway Cinema building. Turn left, rounding the Radway Inn on your left.

You are now heading into town. You'll see All Saints Road off to the right but keep ahead for a further 250m along High Street until the road forks at a building with a beautiful clock high on its façade. Take the left fork, this is Fore Street.

Beach House, The Esplanade

It's worth mentioning here that Sidmouth has a good number of independent stores, which means that the walk may get a little interrupted if you or your fellow walkers are in any way partial to a spot of window shopping.

Continue for 85m along Fore Street keeping a sharp lookout for a tiny alleyway on your right called Cross Lane. This is just before Trumps Grocers. Turn right down here to emerge at the attractive, pedestrianised Old Fore Street.

Although our route essentially turns left here it's worth going right for 70m or so to admire the quaintness of the street – and to also cast your eyes on the former Old Ship Inn on the left.

The Old Ship Inn, *with its stout cob walls and ancient air, dates back to 1350 and was once a den of smuggling – a path leads from the back of the inn to the church which was a possible route for contraband and escaping smugglers. The Inn was also a destination for farmers on market days when its stabling housed their horses while they imbibed. The building may have once served as a monastery. Until recently it had the distinction of being the oldest pub in Sidmouth. A blue plaque outside tells us that 'by the 19thC it had become a notorious Doss House for Vagrants'. At the time of writing it's a Costa Coffee*

Tudor Cottage   Church of St. Giles and St. Nicholas

Return along Old Fore Street, passing Cross Lane again on your left, until you arrive at a broad meeting of ways with Sidmouth Market building on the left. This area has been a centre for trade for generations. Just prior to the market building take the left turn, New Street, passing the old shop front of A. J. Mountstephen, a watchmaker's established in 1902.

At the end of New Street turn right onto Fore Street once again. Continue along here for 40m taking the 2nd right, Kings Lane. Look out for the back wall of the Beach House on your left, one of the notable properties you passed earlier along The Esplanade.

At the end of Kings Lane turn right heading back towards the market, noticing a blue plaque on a left-hand wall indicating that this was formerly part of the 13thC St. Peter's Chapel.

Once back in The Market Square walk away from Sidmouth Market passing Fields department store on your left and continuing along Church Street. Before you reach the church turn left into Chapel Street towards the United Reformed Church. Opposite this you will see the old Tudor Cottage on your right.

Tudor Cottage: *This lovely building is one of the oldest in Sidmouth and has an extremely varied history, at one time being a Church House (see note in Colyton walk). Originally a medieval hall house, its oldest parts probably date from the mid 13thC. In the 1970s a plank and muntin screen dating from 1503 was discovered under a layer of plaster*

Retrace your steps to Church Street where you turn left to visit the Church of St. Giles and St. Nicholas. After soaking up its atmosphere leave the church by the entrance underneath the Victorian west window and turn right. Follow the path through the churchyard – there are massed graves and yew trees to your right. The path leaves the churchyard through a gateway with a bowling club over to the left.

The Church of St. Giles and St. Nicholas: *The present building is the top layer of centuries of history, successive churches having been constructed here since Norman times. The lovely stained glass west window was given by Queen Victoria in memory of her father*

Continue past the bowls on the left and the entrance to Blackmore Gardens on the right. In summer there are some beautifully-constructed floral 'sculptures' beside this path – look out for them. At the end of the bowling greens you reach tennis courts and here you will see a gate on the left leading to a path between the greens and the courts. Take this, there is a good view from here across to the church and its surroundings.

The path leads to Coburg Terrace, there are beautiful houses to the right culminating in Coburg Cottage. Turn left at the end of the terrace, walking along Coburg Road back towards the church. You pass Hope Cottage on the left and reach the top of Church Street, with Sidmouth Museum and the church lychgate on the left. Turn right, away from the museum, passing Kennaway House on your right.

Keep right as the road forks, passing the putting green (open seasonally) on the right. At the end of the putting green cross the road with care to enter Fortfield Terrace. Ascend the steps and at the top turn left to walk along the front of these beautiful Georgian houses which, over the centuries, have boasted some lofty tenants – blue plaques will reveal their identities.

At the end of Fortfield Terrace continue ahead on the path through Sidmouth Cricket Club. Follow the path as it bears right then left, to go round the attractive, thatched pavilion. Continue past more tennis courts and when you reach a T-junction of paths with the Belmont Hotel over to the left, turn right.

This path leads to Manor Road. Turn left, then immediately left again into Glen Road. This road takes you past some smart hotels, The Royal Glen being where Queen Victoria stayed as a child. At the end of Glen Road turn right, uphill, passing some interesting houses on the left hand side of the road. If you cross to read the blue plaques mind the traffic!

Eventually you pass the Westcliff Hotel on the right. Cross Manor Road and a little further along you will find the steps back up to the car park.

Ford

Floral peacock 'sculpture'

Fortfield Terrace

Ashburton
Distance: 1¾ miles / 2.8km

Ashburton has some intriguing and ancient-feeling backwaters which you might not find on a simple shopping visit to the town. This walk explores these as well as having a good look at the centre of this old stannery town (where locally mined tin was weighed, stamped and assessed for duty) with its many listed buildings and enticing independent retailers. There is ample opportunity for some really nice foody stops too, so allow time to make the most of what the town has to offer. There is a short stretch of ascent and descent to visit the Holy Well, but this is a 'there-and-back-again' bit so you can miss it if you wish.

Start point: The Town Hall in North Street, TQ13 7QQ

Directions to start: Ashburton is located on the south eastern edge of Dartmoor. It is roughly half way between Exeter and Plymouth and can be accessed via the busy A38

Parking: Kingsbridge Lane Car Park (pay & display)

Public transport: Ashburton is well served by buses from: Exeter, Plymouth, Newton Abbot, Paignton, Totnes. Bus operators are Stagecoach Devon and Country Bus. Timetables available online at www.travelinesw.com. Nearest railway stations are Totnes (6.3 miles) and Newton Abbot (7 Miles)

Refreshments: Café Green Ginger, 26 East Street, 01364 653939; Moorish, 11 West Street, 01364 654011; The Studio Teashop, 4 Kingsbridge Lane, 01364 653258

Toilets: Kingsbridge Lane

Nearby places to stay: Gages Mill, Buckfastleigh Road, 01364 652391; Golden Lion House, 58 East Street, 07831 787837

Places of interest: Buckfast Butterflies & Dartmoor Otter Sanctuary, The Station, Buckfastleigh, 01364 642916; South Devon Railway, The Station, Buckfastleigh, 0845 345 1420

Market days: Tuesday to Saturday – Tuckers Yard, Chuley Road

Authors' tip: Consider a steam train ride along the South Devon Railway from Buckfastleigh, 3½ miles from Ashburton, to Totnes (see above). It's a beautiful 7-mile stretch which follows the River Dart

The walk starts at the Town Hall, adjacent to the main car park. From outside the Town Hall turn right along North Street towards the town centre. Look left

Ashburton

as you head down North Street to see The House of Cards, a former gaming house with the four card suits decorating its façade. A little further along is a rather venerable medieval granite archway. At the T-junction, with the museum opposite, turn right along West Street, soon passing the public loos on the right.

> **Medieval arch:** *The Grade II listed building which contains this medieval arch was, during the 17thC, The Mermaid Inn. In 1637 a £4 annual rent from the Inn helped fund the Grammar School, then housed in St. Lawrence Chapel. During the Civil War the Inn hosted Fairfax after his Parliamentarian troops had put the Royalists to flight from Ashburton. The building now, with its painted render, looks quite different to the old stone pub which it once was but the arrangement of windows, doors and chimney is unchanged*

You pass the 19thC Methodist Church on the left, founded after a visit to the town by John Wesley, and the 12thC Exeter Inn on the right. Keep ahead along West Street, passing the front entrance of St. Andrew's Church. Beyond this bear left with the road, passing Copperwood Close then soon after taking the left fork down Old Totnes Road.

Exeter Inn: *The medieval Exeter Inn, dating from the early 12thC is Grade II listed. After the death of Elizabeth I in 1603, Sir Walter Raleigh was arrested here and taken to the Tower of London. James I, Elizabeth's successor, disliked Raleigh and tried him for treason. He was found guilty but rather than being executed he remained a prisoner until 1616. He was then freed but was subsequently beheaded at Westminster in 1618*

Down here continue past two left turns, Stonepark and Stonepark Crescent. There are some attractive stone cottages up on the right and the road leads downhill to a large stone cross on the left. Here you will find steps leading to St. Gudula's Well. Beyond the cross you may wish to lean on the old bridge over the River Ashburn for a bit before retracing your steps up Old Totnes Road to the second turning on the right, Stonepark.

House of Cards

St. Gudula's Well: *There are various possible origins for the dedication of this ancient well. Gudula was born in Belgium in the 7thC and she is venerated as one of the patron saints in Brussels, but there is little to connect her with 'sight', and the waters of this well reputedly aid weak eyes. Neither is she known to have visited the area. Alternatively, 6thC Welsh Gudwal was associated with the south west and did have a reputation for healing the sick. The nearby cross is thought to be 14thC but was removed from the site in the 16thC. It was re-erected here in 1933, its component parts having been used prior to that as a mounting block, support for cider vats and possibly a gatepost on a local farm*

Turn right down here passing some barn conversions on the right and when Stonepark leads to a T-junction with Church Path, turn left. You will soon be following an old stone wall on the left and eventually, as Church Path bends right, you will find a gate into the churchyard in front of you. Pass through here, you will notice in front of you the sad little grave of 10 day old Alan Osborne and his parents. It is an extensive churchyard to explore and the church is very worthy of a visit.

St. Andrew's Church: *This lovely church has its origins in the 12thC but the building you see today is primarily 15thC. Hugely impressive from the outside, take time to also look round the interior with its beautiful stained glass windows and wealth of historic features sitting comfortably with more modern 20thC carvings*

After your visit leave the church by the main porch and walk straight ahead to exit through the large wrought iron gates. Turn immediately right along a narrow path and at the T-junction, with Church Cottage in front of you, turn right again, following the path with the railings of the churchyard on the right. There are good views of the church as you progress along here. At the next T-junction turn left, now following the path between stone walls.

The path soon widens and crosses a stream. Beyond this it continues again between stone walls. When it opens up to the right, giving access to a road, ignore this and continue ahead along the still-narrow path. This is Blogishay Lane and emerges onto St. Lawrence Lane. Go left here for just a short distance to see the Chapel of St. Lawrence on the right. After this, return along St. Lawrence Lane, passing Blogishay Lane on the right, shortly after which you turn left. This is Vealenia Terrace, although nothing tells you, and there are some rather attractive town cottages on the left.

Town Hall

St. Andrew's Church

St. Lawrence Chapel

St. Lawrence Chapel *was originally a private chapel for the Bishop of Exeter. In the early 14thC it was given to the town by Bishop Stapledon and became a Chantry School which then evolved into the Grammar School. This closed in 1938 when numbers dropped but was still used as a school annex. It has also been a library and museum. Ashburton retains certain forms of civic administration, such as Court Leet and Court Baron, which date back to Saxon times. The Court Leet elects a portreeve (the steward of a market town) and bailiff who are appointed at an annual ceremony in the chapel*

As the road bends right, glance to the left up picturesque Woodland Road, but continue to the right as the road bends into Whistley Hill. Just beyond the bend is a path on the left signed as Public Footpath, Love Lane. Take this. You pass a school on the right, keep ahead on the broad tarmac path between walls. This narrows, keep straight on. At a T-junction, with a house called Woodlands ahead of you, go left (heading away from the main road) and follow the path, Hares Lane, until it emerges onto East Street. Turn right towards the war memorial. This is an area with some beautiful residential buildings and notice also the large stone mounting block outside the gates of the 20thC Catholic Church.

Turn away from the war memorial and walk back down East Street towards the town centre. You will see Ireland House over on the right, once-residence of

Ireland House

The Golden Lion

the Grammar School headmasters and given to the school governors by John Ireland, a former pupil. Further down on the left is The Golden Lion. On the opposite side of the road to The Golden Lion notice the large stone structure inscribed 'DHBT' and '1974', This is an early 18thC 'conduit head' which once supplied water to the town and which is now a Grade II* listed building. It was restored by the Devon Historic Buildings Trust. Just beyond here, on the right hand side, the pavement widens. Glance back to notice the ancient windows in the building which faces down East Street. There are also lovely views ahead to the fields and woods on the hillside beyond Ashburton.

> **The Golden Lion** *was built as a surgeon's house in 1768 and within 30 years had become a coaching inn. Press gangs would visit here to seek 'volunteers' from amongst sailors who had dropped in to seek solace in ale. In 1984 it became headquarters for the Monster Raving Loony Party and the owner, Alan Hope, became first MRL councillor in 1987 when elected to Ashburton Town Council. The building is Grade II* listed*

Just before you reach the junction with North Street you will find the late medieval Royal Oak Inn on your right. When you reach the town centre turn right along North Street. The walk finishes at the Town Hall, but first go a little further along to admire, and possibly browse in, the building of the Great Hall on the right. This is the old United Reformed Church and now houses a rather enticing antiques centre.

Walk 11
Great Torrington
Distance: 1¼ miles / 2km

This short, easy walk encompasses the historical treats of a town which was a busy place during the English Civil War. Originally a stronghold for Royalist troops under Lord Hopton, Thomas Fairfax brought their stand to an end in 1646 when the Parliamentarian New Model Army took the town at the Battle of Torrington. The walk culminates with some jaw-dropping views.

Start point: Sydney House Car Park, South Street, EX38 8AA

Directions to start: Great Torrington lies 12½ miles south west of Barnstaple in North Devon. The A386 leads into the town

Parking: Sydney House Car Park, South Street (pay & display)

Public transport: Great Torrington is served by buses from many local towns. These are operated by Holsworthy Ltd, Stagecoach Devon and Turners Tours. Timetables available online at www.travelinesw.com. Nearest railway stations are at: Chapelton (6.8 miles); Umberleigh (7.7 miles); Portsmouth Arms Rail Station (8.5 miles); Barnstaple (9 miles)

Refreshments: Black Horse Inn, High Street, 01805 622121; Brown's Delicatessen, 37 South Street, 01805 622900; Café @ Torrington 1646, Castle Hill, 01805 626146; The Plough Arts Centre Café, 9–11 Fore Street, 01805 625925

Toilets: Sydney House Car Park and pannier market

Nearby places to stay: Eastmond House, 4 Potacre Street, 01805 623411; Higher Darracott Farm, nr Huntshaw, 01805 622621

Places of interest: Dartington Crystal, Linden Close, 01805 626242; Torrington 1646, Castle Hill, South Street, 01805 626146; RHS Garden Rosemoor (just outside Great Torrington on the A3124), 01805 624067

Market days: Thursday and Saturday

Authors' tip: If time and energy allow, consider exploring the paths that lead down into the Torridge Valley and alongside the river. This beautiful area has seen little change since Henry Williamson wrote "Tarka the Otter" in the 1920s

In the car park you will see the building of Castle Hill, which is the local information centre and houses the Torrington 1646 exhibition. This area is the site of what was probably an Iron Age hill fort followed later by a medieval castle, hence the name.

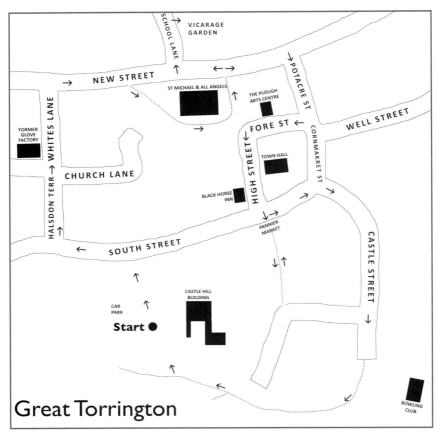

Great Torrington

Leave the car park by the vehicular entrance and turn left along South Street, noting the Sydney House memorial to five children on the left. South Street bends right into Halsdon Terrace, follow this and look out for the striking building of the old glove factory about 100m along on the left The road is now Whites Lane, keep ahead and at the end of the road turn right along New Street. A little way along here enter the gate on the right into the churchyard of St. Michael and All Angels.

Sydney House was built in 1887 by William Vaughan, a successful glove maker and wealthy benefactor to Great Torrington who was responsible, with others, for the founding of the cottage hospital. A deeply religious man, he lived at Sydney House until his death in 1903. His portrait hangs in the museum. Sydney House saw service as a Red Cross Hospital during WWI and later a

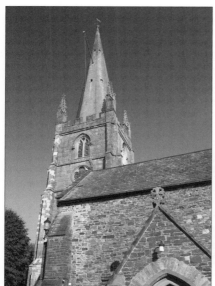

St. Michael and All Angels

Town Hall

The Black Horse and Clock Tower

convalescent home for sick children. The house was destroyed by a fire in 1942 and sadly 5 children were killed

Gloves: *The Vaughan Tapscott Glove Factory was built in 1884 in the style of a Methodist church. The manufacture of gloves has been a major industry for Torrington since the 17thC and continues to this day, though on a much-reduced scale. At the time of writing the building was being sold for residential development*

Visit the church, then turn left out of the porch to walk past a long cobbled mound on your right, this being the mass grave of those who died in the explosion during the Civil War. Follow the path as it bends left round the church to leave the churchyard via a kissing gate back onto New Street. Turn left and cross the road to then turn right in about 25m down School Lane. Just along here on the right you will find access to the Vicarage Gardens which are open to the public but at very variable times. Visit them if you can then retrace your steps back to the kissing gate on New Street through which you emerged from the churchyard.

St. Michael and All Angels: *The oldest parts of the building date back to the 14thC. This church saw great action during the Battle of Torrington in 1646. The ten thousand strong army fighting under Fairfax vastly outnumbered the Royalist troops who were trying to hold the town. Fairfax decided that the church would be a good place to contain prisoners. Unbeknown to him the Royalists had been using the building to store 80 barrels of gunpowder and a stray spark ignited this, blowing the roof off the church, killing the prisoners and many of Fairfax's men. The victims are buried under the cobbled mound outside the church. The church was rebuilt in 1651, and later restored in 1864*

Continue a short distance along New Street to Potacre Street on the right. Opposite the entrance to Potacre Street notice the Old Vicarage. Go down Potacre Street and at the junction with Fore Street turn right again, passing the old post office building on the left and the Plough Arts Centre on the right. Fore Street bends left into High Street, passing the old Town Hall on your left.

Town Hall: *This was damaged by fire in 1724 when many records were lost. It was subsequently rebuilt, the present building dating mostly from the mid 19thC, although the 17thC council chamber does survive. It currently houses the museum*

Plough Arts Centre: *Originally the site of a 16thC wealthy merchant's house which later became The Plough Inn. This was demolished in 1912. The present building dates from 1913 and was built as a Territorial Army drill hall. Artefacts from the original building may now be seen in the museum*

Continue towards the 1870 clock tower, noting the ancient Black Horse Inn on the right. Beyond the clock tower the walk turns left along South Street leaving the town centre, although you may wish to first explore the pannier market beyond the clock tower (after which turn right out of it along South Street!).

Black Horse Inn: *Although this sports the date 1681, an inn existed here in the 16thC and parts of the building date back to this time. It was Hopton's HQ during the civil war. After Hopton's defeat, Fairfax took his place here. The building was damaged by the church explosion*

At the end of South Street turn right along Castle Street. The road bends right, passing the Howe Church Hall on the left, now home of the Torrington Silver Band. As the road again bends right into a car park keep ahead, walking past the bowling club on your left. A superb view now opens up ahead of you across the Torridge Valley (home of "Tarka the Otter"). Here you get a great feel for the fact that Torrington is built on an inland cliff. Keep ahead with the expansive view to your left. Paths do descend to the river, but our town walk stays up at the top of the cliff. Keep straight on until you find yourself walking beside a substantial stone wall on the right.

Follow this wall for about 80m when you will see a gated entrance through a small tower. A little further on is another arched entrance which leads back into the car park from which you started. Go through this arch and turn left, walking along the back of the car park to where you will find an information board on the leper fields in the valley below you. Savour this fabulous view and when you've had your fill seek your car.

Leper Fields: *In the valley below two distinctive strip fields are now all that remain of an old medieval farming system which was used by inmates of the leper hospital at Taddiport (meaning 'toad gate'), the small hamlet which can be seen to the right of the strips. The leper hospital existed during the 13th–14thC and these fields enabled them to grow their own food*

Kingsbridge
Distance: 1¼ miles / 2km

This short walks knits together some of Kingsbridge's historic backwaters with its attractive main street, home to many listed buildings. The town's name derives from a bridge which, around the 10thC, linked the king's neighbouring estates of Chillington and Alvington. Stylish houses now flank the road on the far side of the inlet opposite where the walk begins, giving an elegant feel to the start of Kingsbridge. Spare a glance down the estuary to the pleasant view of the fields beyond the town, the quayside here would once have been a-buzz with shipping and commerce. The paths and pavements are clear throughout the walk.

Start point: The Quay Car Park, TQ7 1HS

Directions to start: Kingsbridge is in the South Hams area of South Devon at the northern tip of the Salcombe Estuary. It is approximately 20 miles south east of Plymouth and can be accessed via the A379

Parking: The Quay Car Park (pay & display)

Public transport: Kingsbridge is linked by buses to the following towns: Plymouth, Dartmouth, Totnes, Salcombe, Exeter, Newton Abbot. Bus operators include First South Devon, Tally Ho! and Stagecoach Devon. Timetables available at www.travelinesw.com. The closest railway station is Ivybridge (9.5 miles)

Refreshments: Driftwood Café, 9 Anchor Shopping Centre, Bridge Street, 01548 852486; The Old Bakery, The Promenade, Kingsbridge Quay, 01548 855777

Toilets: Quayside and Cookworthy Car Park

Nearby places to stay: Auton Court, West Alvington, 01548 857744; Higher Barnfield, 140 Fore Street, 01548 853332

Places of interest: Cookworthy Museum, 108 Fore Street, 01548 853235; South Devon Chilli Farm, Wigford Cross, Loddiswell, 01548 550782

Market days: Tues all year, Thurs from end of March to December. Kingsbridge Farmers' Market – first and third Saturday of the month

Authors' tip: For the ornithologists amongst you a visit to the freshwater lagoon of Slapton Ley is a must. It lies 6½ miles to the east of Kingsbridge and is the largest natural lake in South West England. This Site of Special Scientific Interest (SSSI) and National Nature Reserve (NNR) is only separated from the sea by a fragile shingle bar

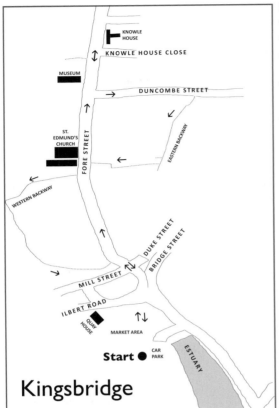

Kingsbridge

KNOWLE HOUSE

KNOWLE HOUSE CLOSE

MUSEUM

DUNCOMBE STREET

ST. EDMUND'S CHURCH

FORE STREET

EASTERN BACKWAY

WESTERN BACKWAY

DUKE STREET

BRIDGE STREET

MILL STREET

ILBERT ROAD

QUAY HOUSE

MARKET AREA

Start ● CAR PARK

ESTUARY

Starting at the entrance to the car park beside the Quay cross the open market place with its large, raised performance area to the left. Beyond this to the left you can see the attractive, creeper-clad, 18thC Quay House, once Twyford School for Girls but now council offices. The TIC is to the right. Walk through the market place, cross over the main road junction, bearing slightly right, to walk ahead up Fore Street, the main shopping road. Within a few metres you see Mill Street on your left and Duke Street on your right, pass these and continue uphill. Ahead you see the spire of St. Edmund's Church and the clock tower on the old Town Hall.

As you climb you pass the 19thC Evangelical Church on the right and the Catholic Church on the left. Originally dating from the first half of the 17thC when it was used by Quakers, the building was extended into a much larger building in the mid 20thC. A little further up on the right is the old Market Hall, notice the names of those responsible for building it engraved in stone by the entrance. Soon you reach the former Town Hall building on the left with its noticeable clock. The building now houses an independent cinema. Just beyond this is the entrance to the churchyard of St. Edmund's which is well worth visiting.

__The Town Hall__ was built in 1850 and now houses an independent cinema. Its ornate clock dates from 1875. The face away from Fore Street has no clock on it. This side pointed towards the former workhouse and it is said that this was a design to prevent the inmates from 'clock-watching'. The workhouse,

The Town Hall with St. Edmund's Church to the right

which was across the valley beyond the churchyard, was built in 1837 and
functioned until the 1930s. It was damaged by fire in 1959 and is now used
as business units

St. Edmund's Church dates back to the 13thC, with some of the tower's
stonework being from the older Norman church. Although many of the very
old features have been lost in rebuilding and successive restorations it is
nonetheless a lovely, Grade I listed church. It wasn't until the early 15thC that
it became a parish church with a consecrated graveyard. Prior to that burials
were carried out at Churchstow, an uphill 2 mile struggle from Kingsbridge. An
ancient door which leads into the Lady Chapel is one of the oldest features,
predating the 1414 rebuild. On the outside wall adjacent to this is the 1793
memorial to Robert Phillip, a local cooper and herbalist who penned the famous
lines which appear on his stone (see picture). A more modern feature is the
1920s lectern on its lovely rough-hewn plinth. The restoration work undertaken
in the 19thC cost £1,300. Pause here and reflect – on inflation if not on things
more spiritual

From here go back down the steps and turn left along Fore Street to walk under
the overhanging Shambles. A short distance beyond here on the right notice, on

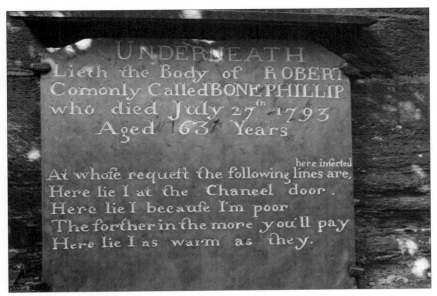

UNDERNEATH
Lieth the Body of ROBERT
Comonly Called BONE PHILLIP
who died July 27ᵗʰ 1793
Aged 163 Years

At whofe requeft the following lines are, here inferted
Here lie I at the Chaneel door.
Here lie I becaufe I'm poor
The forther in the more you'll pay
Here lie I as warm as they.

Memorial to Robert Phillip

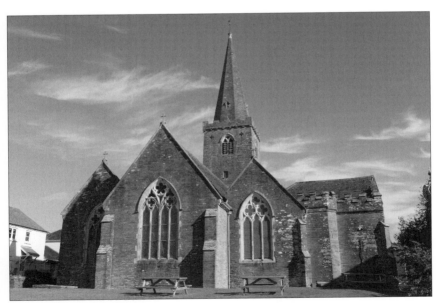

St. Edmund's Church

Fore Street

the other side of the road, the 18thC King's Arms, once a coaching inn, and the attractive multi-coloured, cut-slate façade of the 19thC building beyond it. Keep going up Fore Street, passing the Methodist Church on the left until you reach the Cookworthy Rural Life Museum.

The Shambles *was an Elizabethan butchers' market which was once sited centrally in the street. It was relocated to the side during 18thC road widening but kept 5 of its original granite pillars, dating from 1586*

Cookworthy Museum *occupies the building which was once Kingsbridge Grammar School which was founded in 1671 by Thomas Crispin. A benefactor and first headmaster of the school was William Duncombe – hence the name of the road opposite. The museum is named after William Cookworthy who originated from Kingsbridge and is credited with founding the West Country porcelain industry. A visit to this rural life museum is a must. Focusing on day-to-day living it still exhibits an original school room, a pharmacy and has a wonderful collection of toys, including a gorgeous, button-eyed teddy*

Beyond here on the left is access to the Community Gardens where you can stroll, sit in the sun and buy the produce – call in and, depending on the season, be tempted. After the gardens continue up Fore Street passing its rather smart houses until you reach The Knowle House on the right hand side. Former home of George Montagu.

The Knowle House *was the home of Wiltshire-born naturalist George Montagu who gave his name to the bird he 'discovered', the Montagu's Harrier. He lived here with his mistress, Eliza Dorville, having left his wife behind in Wiltshire. He died in 1815 after contracting tetanus by stepping on a rusty nail in the garden. The British Museum bought his collection of birds. The house is probably late 17thC and is Grade II* listed*

Retrace your steps down Fore Street until you reach Duncombe Street on the left. Turn left here. After St. Edmund's Hall on the right look out for the little pathway on the right called Eastern Backway. Go down here, noting the first buildings you pass on the right – once the cottage hospital. On the left is a car park followed by a playground. Look further left over your shoulder to the tower of the Church of St. Thomas of Canterbury rising above the town.

St. Edmund's Hall, *once known as Oddfellows' Hall, was built at a cost of £1,000. It was originally used as the church hall, for Sunday schools and other meetings. In the late 19thC its basement was fitted out as a gym and games room. It is now residential*

St. Thomas of Canterbury Church *is in the area of Kingsbridge known as Dodbrooke. In medieval times this was a separate town with its own market but Kingsbridge spread and absorbed it. The church is 15thC with later restoration, although a chapel has existed here since the 12thC. The font inside is Norman and predates the existing building*

The Cottage Hospital *was opened in 1898 and was extended in 1918. Depending on which source you believe it had between 7 and 15 beds and its own mortuary. The stone slab on which bodies were laid out still exists!*

The Shambles

Keep along Eastern Backway, ignoring the first turning right which is King's Arms Passage and looking out for the second turning on the right, Wistaria Place. Take this and follow it back towards Fore Street. It winds about and gets a bit dishevelled but soon you emerge opposite St. Edmund's Church. Turn left, cross over and within 50m turn right down White Hart Passage. This bends about and soon you are joined by an attractive old mill leat on the left, harking back to an age when milling was a major part of the town's industry. Follow this path ignoring any turnings off and eventually it curves left to bring you back to the bottom of Fore Street, at which point you find a sign to say that this tucked away backwater was the Western Backway. This is a good vantage point for photographing Fore Street, if you are so inclined. The walk now turns right to return to the road junction beyond which is the market place and your starting point.

Cookworthy Museum

Lynton & Lynmouth

Distance: 2¾ miles / 4.5km

Although Lynmouth is actually a village, Lynton is a small town on the cliffs above it and the two are strongly linked, so we make no apologies for slotting a village into this book of Town Walks. The walk is quite a unique experience: it has some stunning coastal and country scenery and encompasses a remarkable feat of Victorian engineering as part of the route. Occasionally there are short stretches on paths which aren't necessarily tarmac, so flat shoes would be best. There are some ups and downs of gradient during the walk.

Start point: Esplanade Car Park, EX35 6EQ

Directions to start: Lynmouth is situated on the northern edge of Exmoor on the north coast. It can be accessed via the A39

Parking: Esplanade Car Park (pay & display)

Public transport: Buses call here from Barnstaple, Minehead, Taunton and Ilfracombe. Timetables available online at www.travelinesw.com. The nearest railway station is Barnstaple (14½ miles)

Refreshments: Esplanade Fish Bar, The Esplanade, Lynmouth 01598 753798; The Oak Room, Lee Road, Lynton, 01598 753838; The Rising Sun, Lynmouth Street, Lynmouth, 01598 753223; The Vanilla Pod, 10 Queen Street, Lynton, 01598 752460

Toilets: Bottom Meadow Car Park and by the Town Hall in Lynton; Flood Memorial Hall and Lyndale Car Park in Lynmouth

Nearby places to stay: Castle Hill Guest House, Castle Hill, Lynton, 01598 752291; The Heatherville Hotel, Tors Park, Lynmouth, 01598 752327; The Seawood Hotel, North Walk, Lynton, 01598 752272; Shelley's Hotel, Watersmeet Road, Lynmouth, 01598 753219

Places of interest: Exmoor Coast Boat Trips, 01598 753207; Glen Lyn Gorge, Lynmouth, 01598 753207; Lyn Model Railway, Watersmeet Road, Lynmouth, 01598 753330; Lynmouth Flood Memorial Hall (next to harbour)

Market days: A farmers' market is held at the Lynton Town Hall on the 1st Saturday of the month, 10am–12noon. There are no markets in Lynmouth

Authors' tip: Don suitable walking shoes and take a stroll up the spectacular river gorge of the East Lyn to reach Watersmeet (NT). This

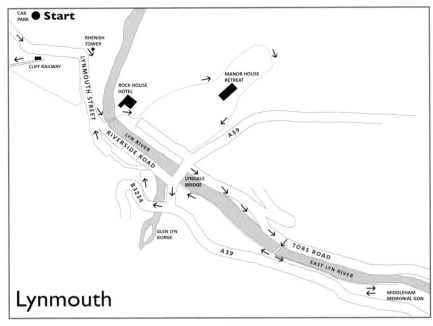

Lynmouth

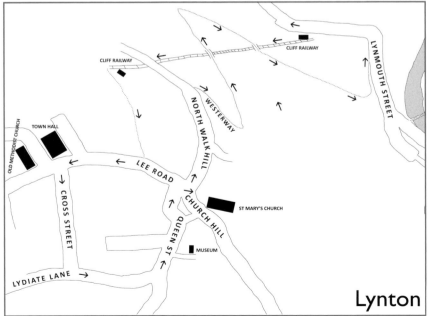

Lynton

Lynmouth

Edwardian tea garden, at the confluence of Hoaroak Water and the East Lyn River, is a perfect spot to enjoy a light lunch or a refreshing cuppa (opening times can vary out of season, it's worth checking before you go – 01598 753348)

Leave the car park by the vehicular entrance and walk along the Esplanade towards the town. There are great views along the coast towards Countisbury Hill and Foreland Point from here. The sea is to your left and you are heading towards the prominent Rhenish Tower. You pass the entrance to the Cliff Railway on your right. Walk out to the tower and from its foot look back up at the amazing feat of engineering which is the Cliff Railway. Its steepness is striking.

> **Rhenish Tower:** *This Grade II listed building was built in the 19thC, a copy of the style of towers found along the Rhine. It was constructed by a General Rawdon and was possibly intended as a beacon to warn boats off the rocks. It was later modified to be a salt water store for use in salt water baths. The tower was damaged in the 1952 flood and rebuilt a couple of years later*

From the tower continue along the main road until you reach a footbridge crossing the river towards the Rock House. Cross this, turning right at its end with the river now on your right. About 30m from The Rock House go left at the fingerpost, signed coast path, heading for the sea. This is a broad, tarmac path so not a problem for the un-booted. Follow the coast path as it bends right past the putting green (open seasonally). Ahead to the right you will see the prominent white building of Manor House Retreat. Keep on the path past the buildings to the right and enjoy the coastal views. The path soon bears right away from the sea, follow it along the signed coast path towards Minehead. Ignore a path left up into woodland but keep ahead on the broad path, passing behind the buildings on the right. You reach a gate by the entrance to Manor House Retreat.

From here walk ahead, crossing the drive to The Rock House and bearing slightly right to where you see a green information board indicating a cross erected on the other side of the river as a memorial to the 34 people who died in the flood. Turn left away from the Retreat and cross the main road towards Tors Road. Go along Tors Road, the East Lyn River is now rushing away to your right. Soon you find a small gate on the right entering a garden to walk beside the river. (Those with dogs will need to follow the road beside the garden as it bends right to meet the gate at the far end.) Those in the garden should leave it via the far gate to continue along Tors Road to the first footbridge.

1952 Flood: *Extremes of weather and climate change are frequent features of our news, and Lynmouth was devastated by one such phenomenon some decades ago. In August 1952, after 9" (23cm) of rain in 24 hours, the already swollen rivers of the East and West Lyn were unable to cope with the deluge. Lynmouth and its environs bore the full force of millions of tonnes of water and its accompanying debris, resulting in the collapse of 39 buildings and the deaths of 34 people. Memorial plaques listing those who died exist in places around Lynton and Lynmouth. One of the saddest aspects of these is the final entry to 'an unknown woman'. Did nobody miss her? Much speculation remains as to the cause of such excessive rainfall*

Turn right to cross the footbridge, turning left at the end of the bridge to descend steps. The river is now on your left. Continue on the clear, well-surfaced path. Within a couple of hundred metres you will see, up on your right, the terrace of the Middleham Memorial Garden, the site of cottages washed away in the flood of 1952. The path gets a little rougher for a few metres between here and the entrance to the garden, but it's worth continuing slightly further to the access path on the right which leads to the garden, in order to visit it properly.

Lyn Valley Art & Craft Centre

Cliff railway ascending to Lynton

Leave the gardens and turn left, back along the river towards Lynmouth. Keep to the riverside path – don't be tempted to veer off – continue past the bridge and the path ends at steps leading up to the road. Turn left along the pavement towards a prominent sign saying 'Glen Lyn Gorge'. Follow the road as it bends right to lead you onto the bridge where you can lean on the railings to marvel at the gorge and the water jet spanning it. This jet is caused by the pressure of the descending river forcing the water through a very small aperture. The curtain of water and, in sunny weather, the resultant rainbow effect, are beautiful. The Glen Lyn Estate uses hydro electric power for its holiday cottages.

Tear yourself away from the view and cross the road, with care. At the left hand side of the bridge railings opposite you will find a small tarmac footpath. Take this as it winds down between walls and houses, looking out for the flood height marker on the left. The path then narrows and emerges onto a pedestrianised shopping street. Turn left.

__The Rising Sun__ is steeped in history. The oldest parts of the building are 14thC, the fireplace to the right as you enter dates from this time and the wonky irregularities of the building are all part of its charm. It is thought that R. D. Blackmore stayed here whilst writing Lorna Doone. The building extends *into what were once fishing cottages. One part of the hotel, known as Shelley's Cottage, is named after the poet who lived in the area during the early 19thC*

Pass through this area of attractive shops and keep ahead as the road passes the Lynmouth Flood Memorial Hall on the left, which is worth a visit for more historical information. Pass The Rising Sun on your left (also worth a visit!). Over to your right you will see the Rhenish Tower you visited earlier. Follow the road as it bends left until, on your left, you reach the entrance to the Cliff Railway. Buy a ticket. Singles and returns are available, although we strongly recommend you descend on foot as it's a lovely stretch of the walk if your knees are up to the downhill gradient.

The Cliff Railway *is a remarkable feat of water-powered engineering funded largely by Sir George Newnes, the wealthy local businessman and benefactor who published Country Life and Strand Magazines. Work started in 1887 by blasting the route up the cliff. The intriguing braking systems were patented in 1888 and by Easter 1890 it was ready for its opening ceremony. Prior to this time any freight shipped into Lynmouth had to be carried up to Lynton by packhorse or cart, a terribly onerous task for the horses*

The Rising Sun, Lynmouth

Lynton's independent cinema

From the top of the Cliff Railway walk away from the station along the broad path, admiring the views to the left. When you reach the road (Lee Road) turn right. You are now in Lynton. Soon you see the rather magnificent Town Hall on the right and just up the side road beyond this is the entrance to Lynton's independent cinema, housed in an old Methodist Church. Adjacent to this in the same building, with an entrance on Lee Road, is a fabulous craft centre. We can't recommend a visit to this highly enough, it's a source of gorgeous treats and gifts. Bear in mind that it closes for a few weeks in the raw months after Christmas.

> **Lynton Town Hall** *was built in 1900 to celebrate the 21st birthday of one of the son's of Sir George Newnes. It was opened by Sir Arthur Conan Doyle and is a fabulous venue for weddings and functions. It once housed the part-time Lynton Cinema before that relocated to the old* **Methodist Church** *where it now functions on a full time basis. Both the Town Hall and the Methodist Church buildings are Grade II listed. The latter, dating from 1910, is the home of Lyn Valley Art and Craft Centre*

From here, stand on the steps and look across the road to the right. Lynton's Cottage Hospital, in a delightful, quaint building dating from 1873, still functions as a part time minor injuries unit together with a police station. You can help it raise funds by attempting to throw coins into the waiting bucket – and presumably making a wish for good health as you do so. Cross the road from the craft centre, bearing left, and go down Cross Street opposite the Town Hall. There are good views across the valley to the left here and at the end of the road you can see the building of the Croft Guest House with an attractive chapel peeping over its roof.

At the T-junction turn left down Lydiate Lane, with its nice old houses and at the left bend, as the road becomes Queen Street, you see the old Public Market building opposite. Follow the road left but then turn right up the side of the market building. This is Market Street and quickly leads to the Lyn and Exmoor Museum, a few metres along on the left. From here retrace your steps down Market Street and turn right along Queen Street.

Keep ahead as Queen Street starts to ascend, noticing the steps to the right which give an enticing view up to the church. Bend left with the road between some interesting shops to emerge opposite the edifice of The Valley of Rocks Hotel. Turn right here, this is now Church Hill, and cross the road to visit the church of St. Mary the Virgin. We had an impromptu organ recital on one occasion that we visited. Those buried in the churchyard have a superb view.

St. Mary the Virgin is a Grade II* listed church and although predominantly 18th & 19thC it has much older roots, the tower dating back to the 13thC. The east window is unusual for not being one window but rather comprising several smaller stained glass windows. In other windows there is a lovely pale green stained glass which gives a light interior

If you have time to sample the Lynton eateries there are many to choose from. Those wishing to descend back to Lynmouth via the railway should walk along Lee Road from the church, to the path which leads back to the station. Those walking down should turn immediately right out of the churchyard to head down North Walk Hill. Pass the entrance to Lynton Cottage Hotel with its stunning view along the gorge of the East Lyn River and the coastline.

About 100m down North Walk Hill you will find a fingerpost indicating that Lynmouth is a sharp right turn off the road along a path. This is Westerway and is part of the coast path. Follow it down and at the first sharp left, which leads to Fairholme Hotel, keep straight ahead on a narrower path which itself bends sharp left in just a few metres, signed for coast path and Lynmouth. Take this left bend and follow the path as it goes down, making full use of the railing! At the first bridge pause to watch any passing Cliff Railway car and to re-engage your knee gears. Keep descending, using the benches if you wish and admiring the solar-powered lamps and glorious views.

Westerway *has been used for centuries as a route for people and goods between Lynton and Lynmouth. At a time when there were no motor vehicles everything travelled by packhorse or on foot. Horses lugged lime, coal and other provisions from the quay to the town above via this path. Smuggled goods used the same route. The road between Lynton and Lynmouth was built in 1828 after which carriages could be used for access, though this was still tough on the horses. Once the Cliff Railway was built this became the favoured option for travelling up and down*

When you are almost at the bottom you meet an option to go left or right. Take the right option, noticing the chimney at the back of The Rising Sun with its witches' seats – designed to appease the passing witch by giving her somewhere to rest so she is less inclined to come down the chimney and perpetrate mischief. Simone tried one out. A few metres after the chimney take the next left bend in the path and soon you are back on the road outside The Rising Sun. Turn left here and make your way back to the car park from which you started.

St. Mary the Virgin

Okehampton
Distance: 2¼ miles / 3.6km
(add 1 mile / 1.6km if going to castle)

This walk takes you to some excellent historic sites in and around Okehampton. The section to the castle is a 'there-and-back-again' stretch so can be left out if you wish to shorten it. However we would strongly recommend you do the whole thing as the view of the ruins on approach is quite striking and it's a lovely walk along the lane to get there. Access to the ruins is only possible from April to September (inclusive) as they are managed by English Heritage. Okehampton town has some rather lovely houses and historic buildings housing modern shops and businesses. There is a bit of uphill in this walk but nothing too challenging. The lovely cobbled paths near the parish church can be a bit slippery.

Start point: Mill Road Car Park, EX20 1PS

Directions to start: Okehampton is positioned on the northern edge of Dartmoor in West Devon. It is 23 miles west of Exeter and can easily be accessed from the A30

Parking: Mill Road Car Park (pay & display)

Public transport: Okehampton is well-served by buses linking the following towns: Barnstaple, Hatherleigh, Tavistock, Moretonhampstead, Newton Abbot, Exeter, Holsworthy, Bude, Newquay. Bus operators include First North Devon, Carmel Coaches, Western Greyhound, Holsworthy Ltd. and Dartline Coaches. Timetables available at www.travelinesw.com. Okehampton railway station is located at Station Road

Refreshments: Church Court Café, 4 Church Court, St. James' Street, 01837 54236

Toilets: Fairplace, Market Street and Mill Road Car Park

Nearby places to stay: Little Widefield Farm, Northlew Road, 01837 54729; Meadowlea Guest House, 65 Station Road, 01837 53200

Places of interest: Museum of Dartmoor Life, 3 West Street, 01837 52295; Okehampton Castle (EH), Castle Lane, 01837 52844

Market days: There is a farmers' market on the 3rd Saturday of the month at St. James' Chapel Square, 9am–1pm

Authors' tip: This is a great location from which to explore the vast expanse of Dartmoor, one of England's last great wildernesses

Okehampton

At the far end of the car park from the vehicular entrance you will see a tall mill chimney. Head for this, bearing right as you leave the car park and you will find yourself walking through a kind of chicane which leads past the chimney on your left. There is a river to your right. Beyond the chimney the path meets a T-junction. Go left, away from the river, and this leads you out to Mill Road.

Chimney: *This Grade II listed structure is close to the former Town Mill. The area has been occupied by mills for centuries, the proximity to the river being a source of water power. This chimney was constructed in the 19thC to serve a manure and vitriol works*

Turn right along the road and as it bends right you will see a fingerpost directing you to the castle. Follow this direction along the road, crossing the East Okement River, and soon you see the entrance to Simmons Park on the left. This is a pleasant place for a wander, after which return to Mill Road and continue as before. Cross the junction with Station Road and to your right you see the rather elegant, 20thC building of Fairplace Church. The next road on the left is Castle Road. If you are going to view the ruins, which adds less than a mile to the walk, take this left turn. Otherwise, follow from (*) below.

Simmons Park: *Sydney Simmons was born in 1840 in a property which still exists near the present museum. His parents ran a printing company in the town and although Sydney did not always live in Okehampton he loved the place. He made his fortune in carpet cleaning businesses and this enabled him to become a hugely generous benefactor to Okehampton. Among his many gifts were the construction of Simmons Park, which opened in 1907, and the repair of the castle ruins and opening up of their environs for the enjoyment of the public. This site he donated to the town in 1917. He died in 1924*

Castle Road passes allotments on the right hand side and later bends right across the river, after which it immediately turns left to follow the river on your left. Keep going and less than half a mile from the town you will see the statuesque castle ruins above you on the hillside. After your visit and exploration retrace your steps to Fairplace Church.

Okehampton Castle

Okehampton Castle *is a very splendid ruin which is Grade I listed. Originally an 11thC motte and bailey castle built after the Norman Conquest, in the 14thC it became a well-appointed residence for the Courtenay family, the Earls of Devon. Towards the middle of the 16thC the family fell from royal grace and Henry Courtenay was beheaded at the Tower of London in 1539. The castle was less frequently occupied after that and fell into ruin. Most of what we see today is the surviving 14thC fabric with some later work. The castle has never seen any battles or skirmishes but it is allegedly haunted by Lady Howard, a black dog and various others*

(*) With Fairplace Church over to the right cross over the road and walk along Fairplace Terrace (if coming from the castle this is effectively straight on). This is St. James' Street and it leads you to the gem of St. James' Chapel.

St. James' Chapel *is a delightful little place licensed by the Pope in 1178 as a chantry chapel to the main parish church. It is a Grade II* listed 'ecumenical chapel', i.e. non-denominational, and belongs to the people of Okehampton. The arches of the arcade on the left, which you can see as you walk through the nave, were built to provide for a later enlargement which never happened. The chapel was rebuilt in the 14thC and the tower dates from this time. A later rebuild took place in 1862. The Westminster Chimes in the clock were installed in 1935 to commemorate the silver jubilee of George V and still chime every quarter of an hour*

Emerge from the chapel through the door at the bottom of its tower and walk straight ahead along Fore Street. On the right you will see the entrance to the rather quaint shopping area of Red Lion Yard. Beyond here, turn right down Market Street, noticing the grand Town Hall building on the corner. The pavement along Market Street is best on the left, so stay safe on that side and keep going as the road bends left uphill at which point look out for the old toll house over on the right.

The Town Hall *is Grade II* listed and dates from 1685. It was built as a private house and in 1740 was bought by the Luxmoore family who owned it until the first half of the 19thC after which it became the Town Hall. The former Town Hall on Middle Row was then demolished*

Soon you reach Ranelagh Road on the left with another lovely toll house, the Bus House, on the corner. Turn left here and follow Ranelagh Road as far as Church Path (not Church Meadow, which comes first!) on the right. Turn along

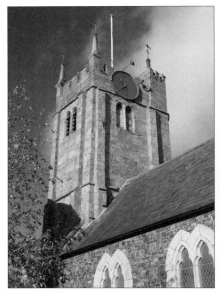

St. James' Chapel

Impressive carvings, St. James' Chapel

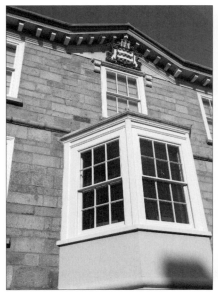

Town Hall

All Saints' Parish Church

Museum courtyard

Church Path which becomes cobbled and leads to a rather gothicky kissing gate. Follow the path beyond here and just before gates onto the road go up the steps on the left onto the Choirboys' Path.

Toll houses: *Several old toll houses still exist around Okehampton and the Bus House is a lovely example. Dating from 1760 it was built by the Okehampton Turnpike Trust to collect fees from those using the turnpike roads. In 1830 it would have cost you 10 old pennies (4p) to drive 20 cattle past here. Vehicles drawn by 6 horses would have had to pay 3 shillings (15p). The conical roof would once have been thatched*

The path emerges onto the road. Cross over and walk ahead to the lychgate of All Saints' Church. After exploring, leave the churchyard via a different lychgate at the end of the path from the main entrance – you know you have the correct one if it's followed by a second lychgate into an extension of the churchyard on the opposite side of the lane. Turn left along the lane, passing a substantial stone mounting block on the left. About 30m along the lane you reach a junction. Keep ahead here along a quiet country lane with lovely views across the town to your left. About 300m from the church you reach a T-junction with Old Road. Turn left. You are now walking downhill with views over the town. At the junction with Moyses Lane keep ahead. Old Road has now become High Street and you drop to a junction with a church dating from 1841 on your right.

> **All Saints' Parish Church** *was probably situated at the centre of the Saxon settlement of 'Ocmundtune'. Successive buildings have occupied the site, the present tower is 15thC with most of the rest of the Grade II listed building dating from the mid 19thC when it was rebuilt after a fire. The Choirboys' Path along which you approached the church was cobbled by Napoleonic prisoners of war*

Turn left here along New Road. Soon you cross the West Okement River, the 19thC bridge you are on being the replacement for a much older packhorse bridge. Keep ahead, this is now West Street and you are heading back towards St. James' Chapel. Over on the right you will see the entrance to the cobbled courtyard area where the museum resides. This is worth a look round, there are some beautiful, contemporary mosaics displayed and the museum itself is worth visiting.

Beyond here the walk continues towards the chapel. Just before you get there you will find an entrance on the right into an arcade between shops. Go through here and at the end you emerge back onto St. James' Street. Turn left, back towards the chapel again, but this time when you get there bear right behind the chapel to emerge onto East Street at the late 19thC Baptist Chapel. Turn right, crossing the East Okement River, and beyond the bridge you pass the venerable Fountain Inn, a coaching inn which dates back to the 16thC.

A little further along East Street you will reach Mill Road on the right. Turn right here and a short distance up on the right hand side is the entrance back to the car park from whence you started.

Walk 15
Tavistock
Distance: 2 miles / 3.2km

In about 800AD the Saxon settlement of Tavy Stock began to grow in an area to the north east of the present town which developed later around the Benedictine Abbey. The walk has a tranquil start along the banks of the canal with its friendly ducks, before returning to the bustle of the historic town centre with its gracious buildings and plethora of blue plaques. There are no serious slopes and plenty of places to indulge in teacakes.

Start point: Bedford Car Park, PL19 8AT

Directions to start: Tavistock is situated in West Devon on the western edge of Dartmoor. It can be reached via the A386 which runs through the town

Parking: Bedford Car Park (pay & display)

Public transport: Tavistock is well served by buses from the following towns: Callington, Plymouth, Launceston, Barnstaple, Hatherleigh, Okehampton, Liskeard, Bodmin, St. Austell, Truro. Bus operators include First South Devon, Holsworthy Ltd, D A C Coaches and Tavistock Community Transport. Timetables available at www.travelinesw.com. The closest railway stations are Gunnislake (4 miles) and Calstock (4.6 miles)

Refreshments: Browns Brasserie, 80 West Street, 01822 618686; East Gate Brasserie, Market Road, 01822 615665; Robertsons Organic Café, 4–8 Pepper Street, 01822 612117

Toilets: Bedford Car Park, Bus Station on Plymouth Road and corner of Abbey Place and Market Road

Nearby places to stay: Apple Tree B&B, 44 Plymouth Road, 01822 617639; Rockmount B&B, Drake Road, 01822 611039

Places of interest: Buckland Abbey (NT), Yelverton, 01822 853607; Tavistock Museum, Court Gate, Guildhall Square, 01822 612546

Market days: The pannier market runs from Tuesday to Saturday, 9am–4pm; farmers' market every 2nd, 4th and 5th Saturday of the month on Bedford Square, 9am–1pm

Authors' tip: The nearby beauty spots of Lydford Gorge (NT) and Brent Tor are well-worth visiting if you have time. Lydford Gorge is famous for its spectacular White Lady and Devil's Cauldron waterfalls. Brent Tor's views from its summit are well worth the effort

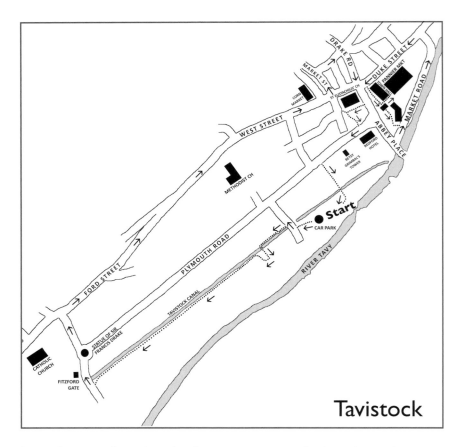

Tavistock

Leave the car park via the vehicular entrance, turn right along the road, crossing the canal, and then turn immediately left to follow the canal on your left. You quickly reach another footbridge re-crossing the canal. Take this then turn right to continue along the water's edge. The canal is now to your right and soon you have a park on the left. Follow this path until you reach a road bridge. Here, pass through the gate, cross over the road when it's safe to do so and turn right along the pavement, first noticing the attractive Fitzford Cottages beside the continuing canal. Go past the turreted building of Fitzford Gate on the left and on the right, in the middle of the road, is the statue of Sir Francis Drake, the first Englishman to circumnavigate the world. It is on this statue that the more famous one in Plymouth is modelled. Beyond the houses to your left you will be aware of the looming presence of the rather gothic Catholic Church. Keep ahead to the T-junction.

Tavistock Canal: *Building work commenced on the canal in 1803. It runs from Tavistock to Morwellham Quay on the River Tamar in Cornwall. Slate, copper ore and many other commodities were transported but use declined in the late 19thC. Unusually for a canal you will notice a distinct current, caused by the fact that the canal slopes throughout its length*

Fitzford Cottages *were built by the Duke of Bedford in the 19thC to accommodate workers from local copper and tin mines. The turreted gatehouse nearby is all that remains of the 15thC mansion belonging to the aristocratic Fitz family. It is one of the unhappy daughters of this family, Mary Howard, who allegedly haunts the route between Tavistock and Okehampton Castle, riding in a carriage made from the bones of her four husbands*

Here turn right along Ford Street, you will notice old almshouses on the left hand side. Keep straight ahead, there are good views of Dartmoor ahead to the right and closer to hand the large, cream-coloured building of the Methodist Church. You reach a junction with a mini roundabout. Keep on, but notice over to the left the attractive white house which was the original Tavistock Cottage Hospital.

Sir Francis Drake

Mystery statue from London

Abbey arch

The 7th Duke of Bedford

__The Cottage Hospital__ was opened in 1887, a gift to the town by Daniel Radford. Nine years later it was replaced by another hospital on Spring Hill

The road becomes West Street. Keep going, looking out for the large statue in the niche on one of the houses on the left. Little is known about who this is, the statue was brought here from London. Continue down the left hand side of West Street with a lovely view of the church ahead. Eventually, at the junction with King Street on the left, you find the Corn Market.

__The Corn Market,__ one of the 6th Duke of Bedford's projects, was built in the 1830s, is Grade II listed and was designed by Charles Fowler who was also responsible for Totnes Bridge and the old Covent Garden Market in London. The building has also served as a cinema

Continue a little further along West Street then turn left along Market Street. Soon you reach the junction with Pym Street along which you turn right, but first notice the building further along Market Street which was the first bank to exist in Tavistock. This was established in 1791 by the Gill family. Over successive generations it expanded and opened more branches outside Tavistock.

Pym Street takes you past the Ordulph Arms on the left. At the end turn right on Drake Road to pass more fabulous 19thC buildings on the left. Soon you reach the open area of Bedford Square. Go straight ahead across the square, passing the Town Hall on the left.

__The Tavistock Temperance Society__ had its inaugural meeting at its new hotel, which is now the Ordulph Arms, in 1838. The building is on the site of the 16thC Great House, one-time residence of the Glanville family. Some of the masonry from this earlier building still exists. The Council later had offices here and it became an Inn in 1983, first as the Sir Francis Drake and then as the Ordulph Arms

Beyond here on the left you find the entrance to the enticing pannier market which shouldn't be missed. There are shops as well as a market so explore and partake, then return to Bedford Square. Continue through the massive stone arch of Court Gate and beyond you will find the old Guildhall and Magistrate's Court and a statue of the seventh Duke. Many of the buildings you see in this area occupy sites once covered by the abbey. Beyond the Guildhall go left along a short path between it and the castellated public loos. This will bring you to Market Road with the River Tavy in front of you.

The Earls and Dukes of Bedford: *After the Dissolution of the Monasteries under Henry VIII, the lands and income of Tavistock Abbey passed to John Russell, the first Earl of Bedford. One of his descendants, the 5th Earl, became Duke of Bedford. Over successive generations the family carried out major works in the town. The Seventh Duke is commemorated with a statue on Bedford Square and it was his redevelopment scheme which shaped this area. The Town Hall is the focal point with the pannier market behind providing an established site for Tavistock's varied produce market. Market trading has been carried on in Tavistock for over 900 years but prior to the pannier market there was a mêlée of stalls throughout the town. The Court Gate arch predates its neighbouring buildings, having been an entrance to the earlier abbey. This Gate has been restored successively over the centuries. Beyond it is the Grade II* listed Guildhall, also mid 19thC but with some 15thC fabric*

Turn left along Market Road and this soon bends left to reach Duke Street. Paddon's Row Shopping Mews is over to the right, should you wish to check it out, but the walk turns left along Duke Street. Notice on the right the Old Folks' Rest Room, commemorating the coronation of Queen Elizabeth II. At the end of Duke Street cross over towards the church, bearing slightly left across Bedford Square to find the entrance to the churchyard. Go in here to explore the area and the church, you will see the ruins of the abbey cloisters over to the left.

St. Eustachius' Church *is quite magnificent. A church was first recorded here in 1265 although none of that building now remains and there is very little left of the subsequent church of 1318, although the base of the tower dates from that time. By the end of the 14thC the church was mostly rebuilt in the Perpendicular style and was then extended in the 15thC. Notice the sumptuously carved oak screen around the organ, created by local craftsmen between 1845 and 1879. Each figure holds a different musical instrument. There is also a grand memorial to the Fitz family of Fitzford. Look for the display case near the main door containing 14thC floor tiles from the adjacent abbey*

The Abbey of St. Mary and St. Rumon *was a Benedictine Abbey founded by Ordgar and his son Ordulph around 965AD. The building was completed by Ordulph in 981AD. It was attacked by Vikings in 997AD and subsequently rebuilt. After the Dissolution, at which time it was occupied by an abbot and 20 monks, much of its stone was used for buildings around the town. The evocative ruins you see today are scheduled Ancient Monuments*

Leave the church and walk out of the churchyard passing the ruins of the cloisters on your right. The Bedford Hotel is opposite you across the road. Turn right along the road and beyond the hotel you will find Betsy Grimbal's Tower. After this continue away from Bedford Square. In about 50m you find a path on the left returning to the car park but pause first and look diagonally right across the road to the building which, between 1837 and 1888, housed the grammar school. One of the first pupils here was W. H. Smith, of stationery fame. On that note, turn left along the path and you will find yourself at the other end of the car park from which you started.

The Bedford Hotel *occupies the site of earlier abbey buildings. Once the residence of the Duke of Bedford's agent (whom he must have held in some regard!) it became an hotel in 1822. The oldest part of the building is 18thC and it is Grade II listed. From here a mail coach went to London every day*

Betsy Grimbal's Tower *was the abbot's residence and one of the great gateways into the abbey. Some say the name derives from the victim of a murderous monk but it is more likely a corruption of 'Blessed Grimbald', a 9thC saint revered by the Benedictines. This Ancient Monument is Grade I listed*

Interior of St. Eustachius' Church

Court Gate

Circular Walks in Central Devon

by

Simone Stanbrook-Byrne and James Clancy

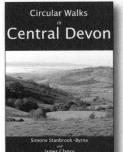

The countryside of Central Devon is often overlooked by walkers in favour of the coasts and moors, but it has much to offer: hidden paths and woodlands, patchwork hillsides and deep valleys.

Having lived in this area for much of their lives, the authors bring you their collection of favoured routes in out-of-the-way places as well as some better-known Devon beauty spots.

More than merely a guide to footpath routes, this book includes details of nearby refreshment stops and local accommodation so will appeal to those holidaying in Devon as much as to those lucky enough to live in the county. Notes on natural history, local interest and authors' tips are also included.

In addition to tempting walkers to explore Devon's heartland, *Circular Walks in Central Devon* will also find favour with photographers who are sure to find plenty of subject matter along these lovely routes.

The Walks

1 Silverton; 2 Cove; 3 Butterleigh; 4 Brampford Speke; 5 Crediton; 6 Culmstock; 7 Oakford; 8 Shobrooke; 9 Thorverton; 10 Tiverton; 11 Bickleigh & Cadeleigh; 12 Stoodleigh; 13 Kennerleigh and Woolfardisworthy; 14 Withleigh; 15 Rackenford

Published: February 2011
Format: Paperback
Pages: 96pp
ISBN: 978-1-907942-01-3

Dimensions: 210x148mm
Publisher: Culm Valley Publishing

Price: £ 6.99

Orders can be placed at www.culmvalleypublishing.co.uk
or, alternatively, by telephone on 01884 849085

A Dozen Dramatic Walks in Devon

by

Simone Stanbrook-Byrne and James Clancy

These twelve circular routes, which incorporate some of Devon's most stunning scenery, are for walkers who like drama, amazing views and a sense of accomplishment at the end of the day.

Taking in some of Devon's most beautiful landscapes, this guide is primarily aimed at those who don't mind putting a little effort into their day's walking. However, options on shorter or easier routes are given where practical for those who prefer less of a challenge.

Encompassing the best of what Devon has to offer, this book introduces the walker to glorious coastline, expansive moorland and deep gorges, as well as gentle, picturesque river valleys and idyllic villages.

More than just a walking guide, each route includes details of local watering holes for refreshment, places to stay and nearby places of interest. Historic notes, authors' tips and pointers on natural history are also included.

A Dozen Dramatic Walks in Devon will also appeal to photographers who are sure to find plenty of subject matter along these fabulous routes.

The exceptional photography which accompanies each walk tempts the reader to venture out and share the authors' love of Devon's great outdoors.

The Walks

1 Drewsteignton & the Teign Gorge 2 Noss Mayo & The Warren 3 Little Switzerland 4 Meldon & the High Tors 5 Trentishoe & the Heddon Valley 6 North Devon's Glorious Beaches 7 Exotic East Portlemouth 8 The Doone Valley 9 Bolt Head & Soar Mill Cove 10 Bigbury-on-Sea & Burgh Island 11 Tavy Cleave 12 Branscombe & the Hooken Undercliff

Published: January 2011
Format: Paperback
Pages: 88pp
ISBN: 978-1-907942-00-6

Dimensions: 210x148mm
Publisher: Culm Valley Publishing

Price: £ 5.99

Orders can be placed at www.culmvalleypublishing.co.uk or, alternatively, by telephone on 01884 849085

A Dozen Dramatic Walks in Somerset

by

Simone Stanbrook-Byrne and James Clancy

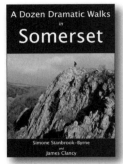

A Dozen Dramatic Walks in Somerset entices walkers to sample the amazing landscapes which Somerset has to offer: spectacular gorges, the wildness of high moorland with its contrasting combes, glorious coastline, picturesque valleys and pretty villages. It is aimed at walkers who like to feel a sense of achievement at the end of a day well-spent in the great outdoors.

More than just a walking guide, these twelve circular routes include details of local refreshment stops, places to stay and nearby places of interest. Historic notes, authors' tips and natural history pointers are also included.

This beautifully-illustrated book will find favour with photographers seeking a wide variety of subject matter, from vast land- and seascapes which change with the seasons to detailed botanical studies. It will appeal as much to those who live in and love Somerset as to those visiting the region.

The Walks

1 Winsford & the Punchbowl 2 West Quantoxhead & the North Quantocks 3 Dunkery Beacon & the Draper's Way 4 Ebbor Gorge 5 Bossington 6 Simonsbath & the Barle Valley 7 Cheddar Gorge 8 Burrington Combe 9 Cadbury Castle & Corton Denham 10 Blagdon Hill 11 County Gate, Exmoor 12 Cothelstone & the South Quantocks

Published: April 2011
Format: Paperback
Pages: 88pp
ISBN: 978-1-907942-02-0

Dimensions: 210x148mm
Publisher: Culm Valley Publishing

Price: £ 5.99

Orders can be placed at www.culmvalleypublishing.co.uk
or, alternatively, by telephone on 01884 849085

A Dozen Dramatic Walks in Cornwall

by

Simone Stanbrook-Byrne and James Clancy

Walkers are spoilt for choice in Cornwall. The aim of this book is to take you to the most spectacular scenery the county has to offer. Magnificent coastline and wild moorland contrast with delightful villages and pockets of verdant woodland.

A Dozen Dramatic Walks in Cornwall guides you on twelve outstanding circular routes.

Stunning photography and clear route instructions, together with details of local refreshment stops, places to stay and nearby places of interest, are all designed to make for the ultimate day out.

History notes, authors' tips and pointers on natural history are also included.

The Dozen Dramatic Walks series finds great favour with photographers who discover plenty of subject matter along these superb routes.

The Walks

1 Trebarwith Strand & Tintagel 2 Bodinnick & the Fowey estuary 3 St. Anthony Head 4 Lizard & Kynance Cove 5 Helford River & Frenchman's Creek 6 Polzeath 7 Treen & Porthcurno 8 Zennor 9 Talland Bay & Polperro 10 Bodmin Moor & the Cheesewring 11 Boscastle & Rocky Valley 12 Chapel Porth, St. Agnes Head & Trevaunance Cove

Published: July 2011
Format: Paperback
Pages: 88pp
ISBN: 978-1-907942-03-7

Dimensions: 210x148mm
Publisher: Culm Valley Publishing

Price: £ 5.99

Orders can be placed at www.culmvalleypublishing.co.uk
or, alternatively, by telephone on 01884 849085

Cathedral Close, Exeter

Final stages of the Great Torrington walk

All images used in this book are available as cards and prints from Culm Valley Publishing
www.culmvalleypublishing.co.uk